EVERYTHING
GUIDE TO
FLIPPING HOUSES

Dear Reader,

If you've seen shows like *Flip This House*, *Flip Men*, or *Flipping Out*, you may have a growing interest in house flipping. House flipping has become increasingly popular over recent years thanks to a number of factors, including the success of these shows. But these shows only offer a snippet view of the house flipping process. The real flipping process often takes months, from the time you decide to flip the house, until you sign the selling papers and collect your profit.

This book will walk you through the entire house flipping process to help you better understand what is involved. You will learn more about the potential benefits house flipping provides, as well as the potential risks involved.

House flipping is a reasonable way to earn extra income or to replace your current income. It provides you with better control over your financial future, and it does not require formal educational training. While there is a learning curve to making the most profit off each flip, what you need to know can be learned through research, talking to mentors, and on-the-job training.

Melanie Williamson

Welcome to the EVERYTHING® Series!

These handy, accessible books give you all you need to tackle a difficult project, gain a new hobby, comprehend a fascinating topic, prepare for an exam, or even brush up on something you learned back in school but have since forgotten.

You can choose to read an Everything® book from cover to cover or just pick out the information you want from our four useful boxes: e-questions, e-facts, e-alerts, and e-ssentials.

We give you everything you need to know on the subject, but throw in a lot of fun stuff along the way, too.

We now have more than 400 Everything® books in print, spanning such wide-ranging categories as weddings, pregnancy, cooking, music instruction, foreign language, crafts, pets, New Age, and so much more. When you're done reading them all, you can finally say you know Everything®!

QUESTION

Answers to
common questions

FACT

Important snippets
of information

ALERT

Urgent
warnings

ESSENTIAL

Quick
handy tips

PUBLISHER Karen Cooper

MANAGING EDITOR, EVERYTHING® SERIES Lisa Laing

COPY CHIEF Casey Ebert

ASSISTANT PRODUCTION EDITOR Alex Guarco

ACQUISITIONS EDITOR Hillary Thompson

ASSOCIATE DEVELOPMENT EDITOR Eileen Mullan

EVERYTHING® SERIES COVER DESIGNER Erin Alexander

Visit the entire Everything® series at *www.everything.com*

THE
EVERYTHING®
GUIDE TO
FLIPPING HOUSES

An all-inclusive guide to:
Buying · Renovating · Selling

Melanie Williamson

Avon, Massachusetts

This book is dedicated to the memory of Russ Harkins.
He was a masterful house flipper and an amazing dad.

Published by
Adams Media, a division of F+W Media, Inc.
57 Littlefield Street, Avon, MA 02322. U.S.A.
www.adamsmedia.com

ISBN 10: 1-4405-8378-1
ISBN 13: 978-1-4405-8378-0
eISBN 10: 1-4405-8379-X
eISBN 13: 978-1-4405-8379-7

Printed in the United States of America.

10 9 8 7 6 5 4 3 2

Library of Congress Cataloging-in-Publication Data

Williamson, Melanie,
  The everything guide to flipping houses / Melanie
Williamson.
    pages cm
  Includes index.
  ISBN 978-1-4405-8378-0 (pb) -- ISBN 1-4405-8378-1 (pb) --
ISBN 978-1-4405-8379-7 (ebook) -- ISBN 1-4405-8379-X (ebook)
  1. Real estate investment--United States. 2. House buying--
United States. 3. House selling--United States. 4. Dwellings--
Remodeling--United States. I. Title.
  HD255.W546 2015
  333.33'830973--dc23
                    2014033504

Cover images © alexmillos/Borys Shevchuk/Kittisak
Taramas/Justin Roque/123RF.

*This book is available at quantity discounts for bulk purchases.
For information, please call 1-800-289-0963.*

Contents

Acknowledgments

I would like to thank Susan Giddings for her help and support putting together the research for this book, and Peter Giddings for his help and insight on green renovations.

Top Ten Advantages of House Flipping

1. Financial freedom

2. Being your own boss

3. Being able to work with your hands

4. Having creative freedom over a large project

5. Being able to give back to a local community

6. Taking something rundown and abandoned, and making it beautiful and useful again

7. Learning new things every day

8. Having the opportunity to network with local investors and prominent community members

9. Starting a new venture with daily risks and excitement

10. Being able to try something new and take a chance on yourself

Introduction

House flipping has had its ups and downs in the media. While it went through a period of wild success when all the market factors were working in favor of the investors, things have since slowed down a bit. After the market crash in 2008, there was a glut of houses on the market and house flippers found themselves unable to sell the properties they had already invested in. However, the negative effects of the housing crash have subsided, and the property investment market is picking up again. Even the Federal Housing Administration (FHA) has made changes to their rules to encourage property investors to flip more houses. These changes include lifting some of the restrictions in place for getting an FHA loan to flip a house.

Flipping houses provides the perfect opportunity to work hard and make an investment in yourself. You can do it as a side business or drop everything and try it full-time. While there are risks, there is a great potential for profit in house flipping. This book provides an overview of house flipping and everything you need to know to get started. The process of flipping a house is not a "get rich quick scheme" or a "get rich with no work" operation. House flippers work hard to accomplish their goals. They have a strong team of people they work with to accomplish those goals, and they are driven.

There is a learning curve when you first start. Don't be surprised if you make some significant mistakes on your first flip, but if you are focused and willing to learn from your mistakes, you can create a profitable business. You can be your own boss and control your own income. You can create financial freedom. This isn't to say there aren't risks and disadvantages to house flipping; there are. You are going to work long hours. You are going to find yourself paying a lot more taxes, and it will be stressful at times. However, it can also be amazingly rewarding.

Learning the basics, gaining an understanding of the real estate business, and finding a mentor are the best ways for you to get started. When you find a mentor, or someone who has found success in flipping houses in the past, ask them if you can assist them on a flip so you can see how they handle the day-to-day business. Another way to ease yourself into house flipping is by starting with a temporary partner. Instead of creating a full business relationship, you can partner with someone on one house, and see how it goes.

The information in this book will act as a springboard for your first flip. You can take the information you learn here and go forward. Focus on the areas you aren't already familiar with because they are the areas you will need to learn the most. Acknowledge the areas where you are already comfortable. For example, a lot of house flippers come from one of two backgrounds; they are either handymen or contractors, who know they can handle the renovations, so they are interested in the business side of it, or they are property investors or landlords, who don't know everything about the renovations, but they understand the market. Either way, starting with a base of knowledge is a great way to move forward quickly.

CHAPTER 1

What Is House Flipping?

House flipping presents a great opportunity for property investing. It is very possible to make a full-time living flipping houses. However, it is a flexible enough opportunity that you can flip a house while also working a full-time job. While there is a learning curve for beginners, nearly anyone can successfully flip a house. The most important thing is to build a solid team to work with and be willing to work hard. House flipping is not an easy job, but it can be very fulfilling and profitable.

The Basic Essentials You Need to Know

There are several popular television shows following people who flip houses for a living. Maybe you've seen some of these, or maybe you know someone who is successfully flipping houses, and you may be thinking it is an ideal business to get into. Many people see flipping houses as a potential side income in addition to their regular job, while some see it as an opportunity to make a career change. A simple search online will reveal plenty of "get rich quick with flipping" books and courses to buy.

This is not one of those books. Where there is a great potential for profit in house flipping, there is also a substantial level of risk involved, and the newer you are to the process, the greater the potential risk. While the intrinsic risk does not change, the lack of experience increases the potential risk.

What Are You Getting Into?

House flipping is the process of buying a house with the sole purpose of reselling it for a profit. In many cases, the houses to be flipped require renovations before they are ready to be resold. However, there are plenty of houses out there that need minimal repairs, and can be ready to resell in a short period of time.

ESSENTIAL

One of the must-haves for successful house flipping is being a good estimator. Accurately estimating the cost of renovations will enable you to make a lot more money flipping houses.

The degree of investment and work involved in a flip varies greatly depending on the situation. It is nearly impossible to use one house flip as a standard or example of how other house flips will work out. House flippers can resell the house to a private buyer or another property investor. Understanding the potential buyer can alter the way the house is renovated and sold.

Essential Points to Understand

There are several things you need to understand upfront before looking into flipping your first house. This is the basic knowledge you should possess before getting into house flipping.

1. **The profit only comes when the house sells.** House flipping requires a large upfront investment. You need to acquire the house, renovate the house, and then sell the house before you will get paid. That means you may invest a large sum of money into the property, and you will not see a return on your investment until the house is sold. Therefore, it is important to understand that selling the house is your number one goal. Additionally, you need to have the money available to make the necessary renovations in order to sell the house. Without the necessary funds, you may get stuck with a partially renovated house, which will make it difficult for you to be able to sell it quickly and make a profit.

2. **Time is money.** The faster you can sell the house, the more money you will make. Every month you own the house, you will be making the house payment and paying the utilities. Even if you buy the house for cash, you will need to have the utilities on in order to work in the house, and that will cost you money. Additionally, rented equipment will cost you money the longer you need it. Dumpsters will cost you money the longer you have them at the house. Therefore, the faster you complete the renovations and sell the house, the fewer expenses you will have going into the house.

3. **This is not your home.** First time house flippers often make the mistake of getting emotionally invested or attached to the house. They make unneeded renovations because they are renovations they would want done if they were living there. This is the wrong way to approach a flip. The primary goal is to sell the house and protect your potential profit. Before starting a flip, you will set a renovation budget, and you need to stick to that. Additionally, the renovations you choose to make will be based on what needs to be done and what will add the most value to the house.

4. **Area is everything.** Houses can be flipped in any neighborhood. However, it is important to keep in mind that the area will set the selling price of the house, and the area will set the standard for what your house

needs to be at to resell. For example, if the comparable houses in the area are selling for $150,000, then you need to understand that is your approximate target goal. You don't want to make $200,000 in renovations with the hopes that a super fancy house will sell for much more. You should understand the standard for the area. For example, if every house in the area has central air, then the house you are flipping should have central air.

ALERT

It is also important to remember that this is not your house when choosing wall colors and flooring. It is better to keep everything neutral than decorate in colors you like and risk having buyers walk away simply because they don't like the way it looks.

Identifying the Current Housing Market

Before choosing a house to flip, you need to choose a neighborhood. You need to identify a neighborhood that has good potential in terms of being able to get a good deal on a house and sell it for a profit.

In addition to identifying a profitable market, you also want to identify a housing market you want to work in. It should be a neighborhood that is a comfortable driving distance from where you live since you'll be driving there on a daily basis. You don't want to spend a small fortune in gas just to work on the house. You want to find a neighborhood you will feel safe working in. There are plenty of neighborhoods throughout the country where you can find a house for as little as a couple thousand dollars, but they aren't always safe areas.

Important Questions to Answer

When choosing an area to buy a flip, you need to get a full understanding of the current housing market. There are several questions you can ask about an area in order to determine whether or not it's in a good area to consider a flip.

Is there a glut of houses currently on the market?

A glut of houses on the market means reselling the house will be difficult because there are so many to choose from. However, having a glut of houses also typically means the area is experiencing a buyers market, which means it is more likely you will be able to get a house cheap.

What is the length of time houses are sitting on the market?

You want to be able to sell the house quickly, once it is renovated. Now, a newly renovated house may sell quicker, but you will be taking a risk if houses in the area tend to sit for weeks or even months. It is important to remember time is money in this business, so you need to be able to sell the renovated house quickly in order to protect your potential profit.

Are there a lot of flipped houses in the area?

A large number of flipped houses in one area is an indication of a few things. First, it was likely an older neighborhood, which is going through a process of revitalization. Secondly, it indicates that others have been able to successfully flip houses in the area. These are both good signs in terms of determining your potential success in the market.

Is the area primarily homeowners or rentals?

This is an important question to answer when creating a strategy to sell your flip. If the area is mostly rentals, your best strategy will be to go into the flip by trying to sell to another property investor or maintaining the house as a rental. While it is not impossible, houses don't always sell well in neighborhoods filled with mostly rental properties. If the area is mostly homeowners, you have more options. First, you will be able to sell the house to a private buyer. Secondly, nicely renovated, higher-end rentals go well in neighborhoods that are mostly homeowners. These types of properties are often rented by people that have the monthly income to live in the neighborhood, but can't get a loan to buy their own house.

Where to Do Your Research

You can gather information from a wide range of sources including the County Auditor's website, the local newspapers, and local realtors. The

County Auditor's website is a great resource because it allows you to access public records, which will include any time a house is bought or sold within the county.

Information included in these records should include the tax value of the property and the price actually paid for the house. If you have the sale information about the house from the newspaper, a realty website, or a realtor, you can see how much the house actually sold for compared to the price it was listed at.

ESSENTIAL

While working with a realtor can help you get information faster, you can find all the needed information about a house's public record by doing a little research on your own.

You can read local newspapers and follow local realty websites to determine the number of houses for sale in the area and the list prices associated with different properties. This can help you determine the value of different house features. For example, if there are two comparable houses, except one has two bathrooms and the other has three bathrooms, you can compare the list prices and the selling prices to determine the approximate value of the third bathroom.

Realtor Caution

Talking to realtors is also a great resource; however, you need to be somewhat cautious. Realtors are in the business of buying and selling houses, so it is in their best interest to make an area sound as desirable as possible to potential buyers. As a potential buyer of houses that may otherwise seem "unsellable" it would be in a realtor's best interest to "sell" the area. This is also why it is important to develop a professional relationship with a realtor interested in working with you long-term. You want a realtor that will be focused on finding the houses you are most interested in buying, opposed to the ones they are most interested in selling.

Looking at Comparables

Comparables are houses that are comparable in area, size, and features, so the selling prices for the houses should be similar. These will also be the houses you will be competing with when trying to sell your house because potential buyers will be looking at yours along with the comparables.

QUESTION

What if there aren't many comparables in the area?
When you don't have a lot of comparables to look at, you want to start with the comparables you do have. Then look at house values in the area to see what houses would be selling for if they were for sale. You can look up tax values using the County Auditor's website in most areas. Your realtor can also help you gather this information.

Looking at comparables can give you a great amount of insight into the potential for a house. It can also give information as to what features potential buyers will be expecting. It is important to understand it is the neighborhood that sets the price for a house and that includes the comparables. For example, you can have a 1,400 square foot split-level house with three bedrooms and two bathrooms. A house like that in Vermilion, Ohio, may cost in the ballpark of $80,000–$100,000. Take that exact same house and place it in Evanston, Illinois, and it will cost $450,000–$500,000. The house is the same; the area dictates the price.

The comparables will show you both the potential selling price for the area, as well as the features the potential buyers will be expecting. This is where it will be important to note if all the comparables have similar features like central air, a pool, a master bathroom, granite countertops, etc.

Short- and Long-Term Benefits

There are many potential benefits of house flipping, both short- and long-term. For many, the benefits outweigh the potential risks, but when deciding whether or not you want to try flipping houses, it is important to understand both the benefits and the risks. A full understanding of these will enable you to make an educated decision.

One significant benefit of house flipping is that it gives you more control over your potential income. While with a traditional job, you make whatever annual salary has been assigned to your position, with house flipping, you can make as much as you want to because you control the number of flips you do each year.

Once you get the hang of it, you can choose to do multiple flips simultaneously. And then, once you get a strong grasp on the inspection process and what to look for, as well as the renovation process, you'll get better at choosing properties that will yield a higher profit.

FACT

House flipping allows you to determine how much you want to make in a year. While the risks are still there, if done correctly, you can create and meet your own income goals.

You can also increase your profits if you have a specific future expense. For example, lets say you decide to do flips semi-part-time, and you are doing four flips a year. However, next year you want to take your significant other on a cruise for your anniversary. You can choose to do an extra flip if you want to make some more money.

The more motivated you are to make money, the faster you can make it happen with a flip. Additionally, once you start flipping houses, you can reinvest your money into new houses and cut out the need to secure outside funding. Being able to fund the houses yourself decreases the expenses associated with borrowing money.

Short-Term Benefits

The short-term benefits of house flipping include the short-term payoff. Even though your investment money is tied up for a while, you get your profit all at once. For example, you buy a house for $20,000, you put $29,000 into the renovations, and sell the house for $79,000. You've just made $30,000. You will get that profit all at once when the house sells. Even if you hate the experience and decide to never do it again, you will have made $30,000, which is more than many people make in a year. Of course you still need to pay taxes and whatnot, but you get the idea.

Another short-term benefit is the knowledge and experience you gain during the flip. Flipping a house requires a wide range of tasks and skills. You'll be doing everything from choosing the right property to helping with the renovations and marketing the completed house. Even if you don't choose to continue flipping houses in the future, the knowledge you gain during the flip will stay with you throughout your life.

Long-Term Benefits

The long-term benefits include a lifestyle alternative. While there is a lot to learn to be a successful house flipper, it does not require a college degree or specialized, expensive training. You can learn through your own research, through a mentor, and through "on-the-job" training. While a lot of work goes into full-time successful house flipping, thousands of people are doing it across the country.

Another long-term benefit of house flipping is having autonomy and control. You get to be your own boss. You make the decisions and your opinion matters. While this independence will feel liberating, it will also come with a high degree of responsibility, as there will be no one else to blame if you fail. It will provide you with the opportunity to grow as a leader and decision-maker.

Common Risks You Must Consider

Just like any investment opportunity or new business, there are risks involved that you need to understand before getting too deeply involved. These risks are often financial, in that you will be spending money you may not get back, but it is more than that. You will be risking the loss of your time, as well as your credit. Being new to the industry, your lack of experience puts you at an even greater risk.

Financial Risks

The biggest risk, the one that keeps most people from trying, is the financial risk. Once you buy a house to flip, you're in it. You have to see it through and sell the house in order to make any money or even get your money back. If the house doesn't sell or takes a long time to sell, you are losing money on the deal.

Lack of Understanding and Experience

Lack of understanding leads to major mistakes. No matter how much you prepare for a flip, you won't be completely prepared for any situation until you're actually faced with the situation. A lack of experience or understanding of different situations can lead to making mistakes that can cost money or delay the house from being sold.

While lack of understanding is a significant risk, it's also a great opportunity for learning. Everyone makes mistakes, but the difference between successful people and unsuccessful people is the ability to learn from those mistakes and move forward, more prepared. Even if you lose money on a flip, that does not mean flipping houses is unprofitable or that you will lose money on future flips. There are multiple variables that go into both buying and selling a flip, which can greatly influence the amount of risk and potential profit in the project.

Working with Dishonest or Inadequate People

Another potential risk is working with inadequate or dishonest contractors. Working with the wrong people can ruin a project. You need to find contractors that are reputable, willing to work fast, and affordable. Obviously, dishonest contractors aren't going to disclose the fact that they are dishonest. It is up to you to look into them, talk to people they have worked for in the past, and then make a judgment call.

ALERT

In talking to several house flippers about this risk, there is one common theme. In each case, the house flipper describes having a bad feeling about the person, but convincing themselves everything was fine. It is generally a good idea to trust your instincts if you feel you can't trust someone who you're potentially going to be working with.

Four Most Common Mistakes People Make

While there are risks that every house flipper will face, there are also common mistakes that new house flippers make. These are mistakes made by people new to the business, but these mistakes can be the difference between making money and not making money. They are caused by inexperience, which is one of the most common risks.

Learning Too Much

Some people spend months, even years, reading about house flipping, taking courses on house flipping, and networking with other house flippers. They spend thousands of dollars on educational material, but they never actually take the next step. They tell people they are still learning, and they want to be fully prepared before jumping in. The problem with this mindset is that it becomes an excuse to never act. Instead of buying into more "education," ask yourself how this additional information will help you. See if it will provide any additional insight from what you've already learned.

Not Learning Enough

This is basically the opposite of the most common mistake. Some people get excited by the idea of making money, so they buy a house that needs to be renovated, without first learning anything about the business. Then they own a house without a clear understanding of how people actually make money flipping houses. They haven't developed positive professional relationships. They haven't done the appropriate research on the market or the potential.

Not Looking at Enough Properties

Some people look at a few properties before making a decision. This leads to one of two possible results: they can't find the ideal property and decide it won't work out or they buy a property that isn't ideal because they think it is their best option. When looking for a property to flip, it is important to look at as many properties as possible within your target area. It is better to have too many options than not enough options. This will give you the ability to choose a property that you are confident has the greatest potential for profit.

Caving In to the Fear of Failure

The fear of failure is very significant for a lot of people. They allow the fear of the unknown and the fear of possible risks to stop them from trying. They are left wondering what they could have accomplished, if they had just tried. The best way to combat the fear of failure is to act; do the research and then buy a house. Once you have the house, you have no choice but to keep moving forward.

FACT

Action can combat more than just the fear of failure. Immersing yourself in whatever you are afraid of allows you to dispel the thoughts that are really behind the fears.

Recognizing Your Potential in Flipping

House flipping provides a great opportunity to create financial freedom. However, there are a wide range of variables that can influence your potential. While most of those variables are internal (your ability to focus, stay on schedule, and under budget) there are external variables that can also affect your potential such as the lending and housing market. You need to be able to get houses that can be flipped at a good price, and potential home buyers need to be able to get loans to buy your houses.

Income Potential with Each Flip

The potential profit for each house will vary depending on a wide range of factors including: the buying price, the cost of renovations, and the selling price. As you gain experience in choosing houses, completing renovations, and selling the houses, the more money you will be able to make with each flip. This is because you will learn to choose better houses, get a lower buying price, complete renovations less expensively, and sell the houses at higher prices.

Income Potential with Multiple Flips

In addition to being able to control how much money you make with each flip, you will be able to control and increase your total income by flipping multiple houses simultaneously. Flipping multiple houses requires a high level of organization and managerial ability, so it isn't recommended for beginners. However, once you've successfully completed a few flips, built strong relationships with other professionals, and are ready to take the plunge, you can turn house flipping into a full-time business. You will only be limited by your own ability and funding resources.

CHAPTER 2

Getting Started

For a beginner, house flipping may feel like the opportunity of a lifetime or like the most nerve-wracking decision you've ever made. Once you get the ball rolling, it's really hard to stop without losing a great deal of money. Your feelings may waiver between excitement and fear on a daily basis and that is okay. While many people have been able to make a great deal of money flipping houses, others have failed. It is good to feel a reasonable level of caution.

Understanding the Flipping Process

Although each flip is going to be unique, there is a general process to understand. This process involves five basic steps that have to be taken in order. Trying to take the steps in the wrong order will lead to a great deal of frustration early on.

1. Find the right property
2. Secure funding
3. Buy the property
4. Complete the renovations
5. Sell the property

These steps are the basis for flipping a house. There are dozens of smaller steps involved in each of these steps, and they will be discussed in detail throughout the book. While there is no clear timeline to follow while going through these steps, the general rule is faster is better. The more time you spend on a flip, the less money you will make. You need to take time into consideration when looking at houses to buy.

Find the Right Property

The first step is finding a property. You want to make sure you don't hold out waiting to find the "perfect" property. You'll hear gurus constantly talk about flipping a house in a weekend or buying a flip that required nothing more than a new paint job and making tens of thousands of dollars in a matter of weeks. While these possibilities exist—they are the exception, not the rule.

ESSENTIAL

One place to look for houses which people often overlook is probate and estate sales. When someone dies and doesn't have any family or the family doesn't want the house, it is sold through probate. Depending on a variety of factors, these houses may be sold at a significant discount.

Waiting for the perfect property is really an excuse to prolong getting starting. If this is what you are doing, you need to take a minute to think about why. Most likely you're hesitant out of fear; either of failure or of the financial risk. Take the time to decide if you are really committed to the idea of flipping a house. If you are hesitant for a different reason, it is still important to confront that reason and decide how committed you are to flipping houses. This is not something you can do halfheartedly. You need to be fully committed.

Although finding the "perfect" house is nearly impossible, you can increase your odds of making a good profit by finding a good deal in your target market. Try to select a house that you can make all the necessary renovations on and still make a profit selling it quickly. In most situations, the best deals will be on foreclosed properties that are up for auction or being sold by a bank.

Secure Financing

The next step is to secure funding for the property. There are a variety of ways this can happen. Getting a loan for the property will allow you to avoid putting too much money down upfront. That way, as long as you sell the property quickly, you will have spent very little on the actual house. For many just starting out, getting a loan through either a bank or through a private investor is the only option.

ALERT

How you secure financing will greatly influence your potential profit, so thoroughly examine your options and make the decision that is best for you.

Paying cash up front is another option. You'll be risking more money initially if the house doesn't sell, but you also avoid having to deal with a loan and monthly payments while renovating the house. Additionally, you can sometimes get better deals if you are able to pay with cash. Being able to pay cash for the house also eliminates the need to involve an investor, which means the potential profit for you will be greater.

Buy the Property

Once the funding is secured, you need to actually buy the property. This is a very important step, because up until this point, you can still change your mind about the whole thing. Once you buy the house, you have to renovate and sell it or you'll lose your investment. This step is where a lot of people falter. They never work up the courage to actually buy the house and get started.

Complete the Renovations

Once you officially own the house, the next step is to renovate it. This step can take anywhere from a couple days to a couple months depending on the condition of the house, and multiple external factors such as contractor schedules and weather. The renovation process is a very important one and requires the greatest degree of management. You need to make sure the house is renovated in a way that will make it highly sellable in the chosen neighborhood, but you also need to save as much money as possible during renovations to maximize your potential profit when it sells.

Sell the Property

The last and final step is selling the house. Selling the property is when you get back the money you invested and make the profit you earned. While selling can take time, selling as quickly as possible is the best way to maximize your potential profit. Selling the property can be the most intimidating step in the flipping process because it is the most important step for profit-making in flipping houses. While the option is yours, you may have better luck working with a realtor to sell the property than trying to sell it yourself.

Establishing Realistic Expectations

You will encounter problems during a flip. Sometimes there will be major problems and sometimes there will be minor problems, but you need to expect problems, nonetheless. Also, you should understand that no matter how many stories you've heard, the house will probably not sell the day it goes on the market. Every flip experience is different because every house is different.

If It Sounds Too Good to Be True, It Probably Is

The house flipping business is not just a big business for house flippers. The home business entrepreneur and personal development niches have also grabbed onto this growing industry. There are unlimited books, classes, conferences, and programs you can buy to teach you how to make millions flipping houses.

FACT

House flipping isn't the only kind of flipping you can do. Try car flipping, furniture flipping, domain name flipping, etc.

While most of these products probably contain some legitimate and valuable information, you need to be realistic. Any program that promises to make you a millionaire in a weekend is probably exaggerating. While there are such things as "no money down" deals, they are not as common as the "gurus" make it sound. Additionally, since the housing market fiasco in 2008, "no money down" deals are even harder to negotiate.

It is important to understand that house flipping is not easy. While the payoff can be significant, you are going to work hard for that money. This is not a "get rich quick" scheme, and it is not an investment that will practically run itself. You will need to be involved in the house and renovation process on a daily basis. You need to be willing to learn as you go and maintain flexibility to deal with problems as they arise. This business is not for the faint of heart.

Always Do Your Research

Once you have some experience flipping houses and you have a strong team working with you, you'll start to make decisions faster and more confidently. However, when you are first starting out, it is important to do your own research. Research the market, research your contractors, and always understand your options come decision-making time. You don't want to make yourself vulnerable to dishonest people or bad situations.

Crafting Achievable Goals

Your specific goals will vary depending on the house you are flipping. However, many professionals set a minimum dollar amount that they want to earn from their flip to make it worth their time. This guides them as they decide which houses to buy and in setting a budget for renovations. Your profit goal will be highly dependent on the market in which you choose to work. Higher-end housing markets can bring in $50,000 or more in profit. However, the financial risk is greater because the houses cost more and the expectations of potential buyers are higher. In lower-end markets, you can expect to make $10,000–$30,000 on flips; this is still a large range. It is important to understand the area you are working in as well as communicating with other house flippers working in your specific market to craft realistic and achievable goals.

Once you have a goal, you need to find a house with a sizeable difference between the asking price and the potential selling price so that your goal is achievable. For example, if your goal is to make $10,000 on a flip, you need to find a house that has a sizeable enough difference between the selling price and the potential asking price so that you can make the necessary renovations while maintaining a profit of $10,000.

If you find a house selling for $25,000 that needs roughly $15,000 in renovations, but the comparables in the area are selling for $55,000–$60,000—a $10,000 profit is a realistic goal. There is enough room for potential profit in this deal that even if your renovations go over budget, or you have to lower your asking price, you can still potentially earn $10,000 from the deal.

ESSENTIAL

As you gain experience flipping houses, you will learn what is referred to as "Napkin Math." This is being able to quickly work out the potential profit of a flip on a napkin.

However, if you find a house selling for $25,000, but it needs $25,000 in renovations and the comparables in the area are selling for $55,000–$60,000, you're going to be cutting it really close. If renovations go over or you have to lower the asking price to sell it, there is a clear possibility you'll make far less profit or break even financially.

While breaking even may not sound terrible because you still get your money back, you need to consider what your time is worth. Breaking even means you made zero profit for all the time and energy you put into the project. Breaking even is only slightly better than losing money on the deal.

Where to Start

When setting your goals, start by seeing what is realistic for your area. Talk to other house flippers about how much they make on their flips. A realistic goal will depend on how much houses are selling for in the area and how cheaply you can find a house to flip. The profitability of an area is highly subjective and varies from one area to another. For this reason, you can't create goals based on what the "gurus" say or what you learn in a "how to get rich quick flipping houses" course.

How to Achieve Your Goals

Once you set some realistic goals, you need to write out the actionable steps you will take to achieve those goals. Actually writing your goals down, as well as the steps you plan to take to achieve your goals, is very important. Writing goals down makes them more concrete. Placing your goals in a place where you can see them on a daily basis will keep you motivated and focused on achieving your goals.

The actionable steps you brainstorm to help you achieve your goals should include a reasonable expectation of how much money you can make flipping a house. You can also include how many houses you want to flip over the course of the next year or even the next six months. This will give you a rough estimate of how much you can expect to make flipping houses in a year. When deciding how many houses you want to flip in a year, you need to take into consideration how much time you will be able to devote to the houses. This will vary based on your other obligations.

Making a Business Plan

Although flipping houses differs from a normal business with a commercial location, inventory, and employees, it is still going to be a business for you. Having a business plan prepared ahead of time will help you to figure out all the details before putting any money on the line. Creating a business plan is your opportunity to really think through all the details of the business.

In the business plan, you will need to create a budget. The budget will vary depending on what house you buy and how much is needed in terms of renovations. However, you should include your total available budget as this will dictate how much you are able to invest in the first house. If you are still working on securing financing, you will need to do more research and adjust the proposed budget based on the house you find.

QUESTION

Other than presenting to potential financiers and thinking out ideas, how is a business plan beneficial for house flipping?
A well-written business plan can help you deal with displacement. Whenever you do something in business, you don't do something else. A business plan allows you to ensure you are spending your time on the tasks that are going to get you to your goals the fastest.

What to Include in Your Business Plan

Your business plan will include seven basic sections. Each section will require its own research and analysis. The process of creating a business plan can provide you with a great deal of insight into your methods and prospects. Writing a business plan is a specialty within itself. If you are struggling with this step, it may be helpful to work with someone experienced in writing business plans.

How to Create a Business Plan

Create your business plan one section at a time. It will probably be easiest to work through from start to finish. You should start with a title page. For the most part, the business plan is for you; if you need to seek financing, you will need to present it to others. The sections in the business plan are as follows:

Executive Summary

The executive summary is relatively simple, yet a lot of people put off writing it. This can be as short as one page, but it is a basic summary of the report. It clearly states what you are looking for from possible investors. It briefly states what you need the money for, and it provides an overview of your business goals. Your executive summary can be more detailed, but you will be expanding on all the details in the other sections of the business plan.

Business Description

The business description starts broad and gets more specific. Start with a breakdown of the industry in your region. This would include an overview of house flipping in your area, how many houses are on the market, potential profits, etc. From there, you would narrow your descriptions to specifically discuss your business prospects in the area. This can include any experience you have that is relevant to house flipping. Your experience may be on the business side of house flipping or on the renovation side. Any experience you have is relevant. You can also include a description of others you've already spoken with who will be a resource for you in the future. This may include a realtor, lawyer, accountant, contractors, etc.

Marketing Strategies

Typically, the marketing strategy section describes how you plan to market your business. However, you don't exactly need to market yourself as a house flipper. Instead, you can focus on your strategies for selling the houses you renovate. Since selling the houses is essential to the profitability of this business venture, you need to give in-depth thought to your marketing and selling strategies. This is a very important section, and prospective investors will want to know how you plan to sell the houses.

Competitive Analysis

The competitive analysis should focus on two things. First, is the competition coming from other house flippers. Are there a lot in your area? Is it hard to get a good deal on houses because there are so many people trying to buy? These are things you should know prior to jumping in the market. The second area to focus on is the competition in the housing market. Are you located in a buyer's market or a seller's market? What competition will you have when trying to sell your houses?

Design and Development Plan

This section is not as important because you aren't working to develop an actual product. However, if you plan to launch a full-fledged business, you can use this section to discuss how you plan to create and develop your brand. This will include a business name, logo, marketing material, etc. You want to keep your options open, even if you plan on starting small.

Once again, this may not be needed depending on your goals. If you are planning to flip a couple of houses while maintaining your full-time job, there is no real need for you to have a brand. However, if you are planning to launch a business around your house flipping, you will want to create a brand. This may mean becoming a full-time house flipper, or it could mean expanding your brand into buying and selling rental properties, property management, etc.

There are many facets to property investing, and a lot of professionals in the field have overlapping "jobs." For example, there is a company in Lorain County, Ohio, called Realty Trust Services. The owners of this company, Steve and Kari Taylor, started out as landlords, but saw a need in their area for property management and maintenance. They established themselves as a brand and expanded into managing and maintaining other investor's properties. They are actively involved with the local property investor's professional organization, and they have created a networking hub. If you are buying, selling, flipping, or renting properties in their area, they can help you find the services you need or make the connections you need.

Operations and Management Plan

This is where you will explain how you plan to manage your business on a day-to-day basis. Will you personally oversee the renovations or will you hire a general contractor? Will you be working on the renovations or just overseeing them? Are you also working another job? Will your entire focus be on house flipping or will you do it in-between other projects and activities? This is the section where you need to be really honest about your involvement. If this is something you haven't completely thought out yet, this is the time to do that.

ESSENTIAL

Developing a strong support network is essential to your overall happiness and success as a house flipper. It is important to seek out networks of people that understand what you are trying to accomplish and support your efforts.

Another important aspect that people don't always consider ahead of time is the personal support they will be receiving. House flipping doesn't only happen Monday through Friday from 9:00 A.M. to 5:00 P.M. When you are pushing to get a house on the market and working around contractor's schedules, you will put in plenty of evening and weekend hours. This can take a toll on family and personal relationships. If there is a significant other in your life, you want to make sure they fully understand the level of commitment needed to make house flipping successful.

Financial Factors

The financial factors are the last section in your plan, but certainly not less important than the other areas; particularly if you are seeking out financing. This is where you need to detail how much you are personally able to invest, how much money you are going to need, how much you plan to make flipping houses, etc. This is the area where you need to look at real numbers, not just hypotheticals. Considering the houses that are currently available that need renovations, what prices are you looking at? You can come up with a purchasing range based on the range of prices in your target market.

Setting Project Parameters

You also need to set time parameters for your projects. While things can change, you always want to start with a solid plan, which includes a timeline. Additionally, you should begin your project with time parameters in mind. For example, you can decide you will not buy any houses that will take longer than four weeks to renovate. This means you will be able to flip houses approximately every two months, if you do one at a time.

Creating a Timeline

You need to have two overlapping timelines in mind. First, there is the total timeline that will include the time it takes to buy and sell a property. There is also the renovation timeline that will detail the needed renovations and how long they will take. For example, if you have a six-week renovation timeline, your total timeline will be more like twelve weeks. This gives you six weeks to buy and sell the property. You may not need six weeks, but if you plan for it, you will not have to worry about going over your deadline.

What Factors to Consider

When creating the timeline, you need to factor in what renovations are needed, and whether they will be completed by contractors or if you are doing them yourself. Although you want to make sure progress is being made every day, you also want to be realistic. If you are working with contractors, talk to your contractors about how much time they will need to complete the job. You will also need to take into consideration the current selling market. Find out the average time houses are in your particular market before they sell. While it is always good to be optimistic, it would be unrealistic to assume your house is going to sell significantly faster than all the other houses in your particular market.

ESSENTIAL

You also need to take the weather into consideration. If you have exterior renovations to do, you need the weather to cooperate with you. Sometimes the things that will delay your schedule will be completely out of your control, and you need to be prepared for that. Watch The Weather Channel each day, so you can make changes to your schedule as needed.

Sticking to Your Timeline

There are several things you can do to stay on schedule with your house flip. The first thing is be prepared to stay in consistent contact with everyone. Don't be afraid to call your contractors to request updates. Being at the property on a regular basis is also essential. This will allow you to be on top of things so you can make the needed adjustments if things aren't going right.

You also need to schedule work to be done simultaneously, whenever possible. For example, getting new carpeting installed will not impact new siding being put up, so you can schedule those projects to be done simultaneously. While other projects should be staggered. For example, you should not schedule the carpets to be installed the same week the contractors are fixing water damage on the ceilings. These two projects would interfere with one another.

CHAPTER 3

Securing Project Funding

There are many options in project funding. Lack of personal financing should not be a reason to drop the idea of house flipping. However, you should prepare to bring a realistic amount of needed funds and resources. The costs associated with flipping only start with the acquisition cost of the house. You also need to figure in the costs of renovations, fees, permits, and contractors.

Estimating Costs

One of the biggest mistakes new flippers make is not properly estimating the cost of renovating the house they bought. The total costs of flipping includes the costs of acquiring the house and the cost of renovating the house. A budget can't be made until after the costs are properly estimated for the renovations. This is why the inspection process is so important.

During the inspection, you are writing down all the problems with the house; big and small. Even something as small as the front of the house needing new downspouts is going to take time and cost money, so it needs to be figured in when estimating costs.

ALERT

Another big mistake new house flippers make is not starting with enough money to finish the flip. They underestimate their needs, which results in them not being able to complete the renovations or having to cut corners and sell the house for less.

Go over your notes from the inspection and make a list of the needed renovations. For the project you plan to hire out, contact your contractors and get estimates from them based on the level of work needed. If you take proper notes during the inspection, you should be able to get approximate estimates over the phone or via e-mail without your contractor having to visit the property.

House Costs

The house costs will include the purchase price, closing costs, house insurance, utilities, and property taxes that you are responsible for while in ownership of the house. You will need to figure out how much you will have to pay in housing costs. While the utilities may fluctuate, the other figures are feasible to figure out on your own or with the help of your realtor.

Renovation Costs

The renovation costs will include all expenses directly related to the renovations. This will include supplies and materials, equipment rental, and contractors. The amount of money spent on renovations will depend on a variety of factors including the amount of renovations needed and how much of the work you hire out. While it may be more time consuming, doing some or all of the work yourself does decrease the total cost of renovations.

Costs of Doing Business

The costs of doing business will include expenses such as your business insurance, accountant fees, legal fees, etc. These are expenses that will need to be paid as long as you are in the house flipping business; they won't be tied to any one house project. Some of these fees will need to be paid up front, like business insurance; while some will be paid later, like taxes and accountant fees. Regardless of when you will need to pay these, it is important to keep them in mind so they don't come as a shock.

When figuring in business costs, don't forget to include things like notepads, pens, folders, envelopes, and other office supplies. These might seem nominal, but if you aren't watching how you spend, you will end up spending more than you realize. Every possible business expense should be factored into the budget.

Creating a Budget

Creating a budget is essential when flipping a house. Staying on budget is how you will be able to protect your profits. Clearly, you can't stay on budget if you don't have a clear budget to start with. The budget and the timeline will be your two most important guides taking you through the flip. It is important to adhere to each as closely as possible.

How to Create a Budget

When you are looking at properties to flip, you need to conduct a complete inspection of the property in order to properly estimate the costs of renovating the house. There are two things to consider when creating a budget. The first is how much it will cost to renovate the property, and the second is how much you can spend to renovate the property. If you only have $30,000 to invest in renovations, then you need to find a property that will cost less than $30,000 to renovate.

To create a budget, you need to start with your list of estimated renovations and housing costs. These are going to be your budgeted expenses. It is best to create your list in an Excel worksheet so you can track and monitor your spending. For every dollar you spend, you record it in your budget under the appropriate renovation.

What Should Be Included in the Budget

The budget should start with your housing budget. It will also need to include any closing costs associated with buying the house. It should then detail the expected renovation costs. This will include estimates you have already collected from contractors regarding specific renovations that are needed. You'll need to include an estimate for other renovation costs based on the cost of supplies and materials, if you are not already working with a contractor on these estimates. Finally, you will need to include the cost of marketing the house to sell. If you are working with a realtor, many of these costs may be covered by your realtor. Marketing costs may include printing color fliers, placing ads in the local papers, getting signs to put in the yard, etc.

When creating your budget for the project, using an Excel worksheet will help tremendously. You should make a list of all the needed renovations. For each renovation, list the estimated cost involved. Don't cut yourself short hoping or assuming you'll be able to somehow save money. It is better to estimate high and come in below budget than estimate low and go over budget.

How to Track and Maintain the Budget

The first thing you need to do is make sure you record every expense and get a receipt for every dollar you spend. This will enable you to keep close track of how much money is being spent as it is being spent. Staying organized and well documented throughout the renovation process will also save you time and energy when it is time to file your taxes. It is important to review and record your receipts on a very regular basis. While daily is best, two or three times a week is adequate.

Another factor to take under consideration is if you are the only one spending money, or if you have authorized the people working for you to spend money. If you have people working for you, there needs to be a clear procedure on how and when money is spent.

The second thing you need to do is keep an eye on your contractors. If a contractor provides you with an estimate and then needs to go over the estimated account, you need to be willing to discuss this with the contractor. Find out exactly why they feel the project is going over budget and why the current concerns were not included in the original estimate. Just as it is important to maintain personal accountability, it is important to keep others accountable for their work.

Finally, another way to stay on budget is to aim high. There will always be unexpected expenses. While it is your job to mitigate those expenses as much as possible, it is not always possible. For that reason, it is wise to add an additional expense to your projected budget for miscellaneous expenses that may arise. If this isn't needed, you will finish the project safely under budget, which means a greater potential profit.

Bank Financing

Bank financing means getting a home loan for the house you want to flip. This will pay the seller upfront and then break the cost down into monthly mortgage payments, which you will have to pay every month you are in ownership of the house. Bank financing will not always be possible depending on the type of property you are buying. It is important to meet with your loan specialist prior to applying for a loan to discuss what you are trying to do.

How to Apply for Bank Financing

When applying for a loan, you will meet with a loan specialist at your bank. You will need to fill out all the needed loan applications and provide any documents requested by the bank. This type of process is really no different than if you were trying to buy a house for yourself to live in.

Depending on the bank and situation, you may be expected to provide a down payment on the property. This is something you can ask the loan specialist ahead of time to ensure that there aren't any surprises.

Advantages of Using Bank Financing

The greatest advantage of bank financing is that it defers the housing expense. You might pay $30,000 for a house, but if you only own it for three months and your monthly payments were $600, you're only paying $1,800 out of pocket for the opportunity to turn a profit on the flip. Going with bank financing will also help build positive credit, as well as a positive relationship with the bank, which may help you down the road.

QUESTION

What if I don't have good credit? Should I look into getting financing from a mortgage company?
Mortgage companies are generally not the best option. The cost of doing business with a mortgage company tends to be higher. They regularly buy and sell mortgages, which can be distracting and frustrating. It is better to work with a traditional lender.

Disadvantages of Using Bank Financing

You can pursue getting a home loan for a flip. This would allow you to buy the house without having to pay for the house upfront. Like everything, there are pros and cons to this approach. First of all, you need to get approved for a bank loan for this to work. More than likely, you will still need to put money down to buy the house. You will be paying interest on the loan, so that needs to be considered when figuring out your projected expenses and potential profit.

Working with an Investor

An investor typically comes in two forms. The first is a silent investor. This is someone who gives you money in exchange for a payback plus interest for use of the money. This type of investor has no involvement in the actual house flip. They entrust you with use of their money.

The second type of investor is a partner. If you have the know-how and ambition to start flipping houses, but you don't have the money or the credit to buy houses, you can find a partner that is also interested and can back the project financially. A partner will have say in what house is bought and what renovations are made. This needs to be a person you feel you can work with one-on-one. Regardless of which type of investor you find to work with, you need to create a legal relationship with your investor.

Advantages and Disadvantages of Working with an Investor

The advantages of working with an investor include the fact that there is the potential for more flexibility than there is with a bank. Banks only operate on one level; they loan you money and you make monthly payments until the money is paid back. With an investor, you can work out many kinds of terms and arrangements based on your needs and your investor's willingness to agree.

The disadvantages of working with an investor can include the personal nature of the relationship. While this isn't always the case, if you work with an investor that keeps tabs on the project, you will be interacting with them on a regular basis. This means there is a greater potential for clashing personalities. You don't have this problem when working with a bank because they don't talk to you unless you are late making your loan payments.

How to Find an Investor

There are many ways to find an investor. You can start by letting people know you are looking for one. There may be someone you are already networking with who would be interested in investing in you or someone you know may be able to connect you with someone interested in investing. Additionally, many investors interested in property investments work closely with real estate agents, so ask your agent if they know any investors. Ask your agent to do a little networking with other agents to see if they can find anyone.

FACT

Shows like *Shark Tank* and *The Profit* have made the idea of working with an investor very popular. However, property investing is different than small business investing. You need to focus on people interested in property investing. Plus, it is unlikely you will find a millionaire interested in funding your one house flip.

If you can't personally find an investor, you can go online. Check out real estate investor websites to look for investor or mentor programs in your area. Go to Craigslist and check the real estate section for ads posted by investors. Ads that say things like, "We Buy Houses" are generally posted by groups of investors looking for local property investment opportunities.

If it's legal in your state, you can also go to investment websites. These types of websites allow you to create a profile with your contact info, business plan, investment amount needed, and what you are offering in return. Investors are able to look at your profile and decide if they want to invest in your project. You may get one investor backing the entire project, or you might get twenty investors funding a portion of your project.

Determining the Investor's Level of Involvement

It is very important to fully discuss with the potential investor their level of involvement prior to entering into a legal relationship. If these things are not talked out, you both may go into the partnership with very different ideas regarding who is in charge of the flip. Some investors will want nothing to do with your project. They just want to see a good return on their investment. Other investors may want to take a more active role to make sure you are accomplishing everything you say you're going to accomplish.

Creating a Legal Relationship

In order to create a legal relationship with an investor, you will need to enter into a contract together. It is essential that you work with a lawyer to create the contract. If the investor creates the contract, it is essential to have a lawyer review the contract prior to your signing it. Relationships with investors can be very complicated, and if the investment is not profitable, they can get even more complicated. This is not a step you can do on your own.

ALERT

Never go into an investor relationship without making it legal on paper. The days of handshake agreements are over.

Funding the Flip Without an Investor

There is also a third option for funding; you can fund the flip yourself or with the help of people close to you. If you have money in savings, you can choose to spend your own money to buy the house and fund the renovations. Doing this may be nerve-wracking, but it will also allow you to avoid jumping through all the hoops of securing financing. Using your own money also means you won't have to make payments on the property while working on it, and you won't have to answer to anyone about the decisions you make.

Getting Help with Self-Financing

If you don't have enough to finance the entire project, you can also ask for help from people close to you. A lot of home business entrepreneurs have started out by borrowing money from someone close to them. While this is similar to getting an investor, it isn't as complicated. Whether or not this person is simply paid back or paid back with interest will depend on your personal arrangement with them. The advantage to this is it can allow you to move forward with the project when other funding sources aren't an option. The disadvantage to this is if you lose money on the flip, you will owe money to someone you are close to.

Reinvesting after the First Flip

Another option to consider is reinvesting your profits once you finish your first flip. You may need to get help on your first house flip. However, if you make it profitable, you will have money to reinvest into your next flip. Reinvesting profits is a common practice in this business. In addition to giving you financial independence, it also enables you to avoid paying capital gains tax.

ESSENTIAL

The capital gains tax is a tax applied to the profit made and kept by selling a property or making an investment. However, if you reinvest the profit you make into another house or investment, you can avoid paying capital gains.

Calculating Potential Profit

The profit on a property is the selling price minus all expenses. Expenses include any money spent to buy or sell the property and all the money spent during renovations. Understanding the potential profit for a property and being able to justify how you came up with that number will be essential when working to secure financing.

Protecting Your Potential Profit

There are many ways you can protect your potential profits. The first and foremost is to keep your primary goal in mind at all times, which is to protect your profits. Simply remembering that will prevent you from spending foolishly on unnecessary materials or renovations.

Setting realistic goals will increase your chances of accomplishing your goals. This means knowing how much you can realistically make on a particular property. Setting goals beyond what is possible is setting yourself up for failure. You also need to be realistic when setting time goals. If you buy a house that requires major renovations, it would be unrealistic to think you could get it done and market ready in two weeks. You need to talk to your contractors, create a schedule, and go from there.

Assessing Financial Risks

The more money you put into a house, the higher the financial risk. This isn't to say you should put as little money as possible into the flip. This simply means you need to be prepared. Understanding how much you stand to lose will make you even more motivated to make the flip profitable.

Understanding the Real Consequences

The consequences at play are more than simply not making money. If you are unable to finish the project or sell the house, you will lose all the money invested. If you bought the house through bank financing, you will need to keep up the payments or risk foreclosure, which will significantly damage your credit. You will also be hurting any contractors that worked on the property if you are then unable to pay them. This will hurt them financially and damage any ongoing professional relationship you may have had with them. Additionally, if you worked with investors or had friends or family invest in your project, you will be hurting those relationships as well.

Mitigating Financial Risk

One smart way to mitigate financial risk is to start looking for a buyer before the house is even finished. For example, you can establish a professional relationship with a landlord in the area where you are interested in flipping houses, who is interested in buying more properties. You can work together to find a property that he is interested in but needs renovation. You can agree on a selling price, and then you can flip the house knowing exactly who you will be selling it to and how much he is willing to pay for the house. If you follow this route, it is best to get everything in writing.

CHAPTER 4

Developing Relationships in the Business

Developing long-term mutually beneficial relationships is essential to your long-term success. Even if you aren't sure you want to flip houses in the long run, developing those relationships early on will give you more options in the future. Additionally, seeking out professionals before you need them will make the decision process easier when the time comes. Once you start flipping houses, timing is important, so you don't want to waste time trying to find the professionals you need then.

Doing Your Research

Developing professional relationships means seeking out other professionals that you trust and feel comfortable working with. Finding reputable contractors, realtors, investors, and suppliers can be a frustrating process. However, with the right research, it can be done. When looking for people to work with, you want to look for people who have plenty of experience.

While newbies in the business may be eager to get their feet wet, they are also inexperienced. This may lead to mistakes that can cost you time and money. If you do decide to work with someone who is new in the business because you were impressed with their eagerness or ambition, it is a good idea to have a Plan B just in case.

Adopting a Team Mentality

While developing these professional relationships, you need to adopt a team mentality. While this is your business and your investment, thinking of it as a team effort will help you appreciate and understand the importance of the people you are working with. When talking to people you may choose to work with, it is important to let them know your long-term plans in regard to the business. If they understand this initial project is only the first of many, they will understand the long-term benefits of working with you.

FACT

Dr. Jason Selk, a contributor with *Forbes* magazine, stresses the importance of adopting the right mentality when going into a new situation. In order to be a winner in business or in life, you need to have a winning mentality.

What Professionals You Will Need on Your Team

You will need a realtor to help you buy and sell the houses, as well as do research for you on the areas you are interested in working in. Unless you are financing the project yourself, you will need a banker or investor to help with financing. You will also need contractors. You can choose to find a general contractor, who will then handle any subcontractors, or you can take on the role of general contractor. In that case, you will need to develop relationships with subcontractors that you will need while renovating houses. This may include a carpet installer, a roofer, painter, etc. If you don't already have them, you will also need an accountant and possibly a lawyer to look over investor contracts.

How to Choose People to Work With

Finding the right people to work with can be an intimidating task. When looking for people to work with, talk to other property investors who have been in the business for awhile to see who they would recommend. Everyone has specific people, and you'll find that there are certain contractors that get a lot of repeat business from property investors. This is because they are reasonably priced, reliable, and understand the importance of speedy work.

If there is a professional organization for property investors in your area, this is likely going to be a great resource for you. These types of professional organizations frequently have vendor members who are contractors, realtors, suppliers, etc., who are specifically interested in working with investors.

Don't worry if you don't find the perfect contractor on the first day. You may need to talk to multiple contractors before you find the ones you want to work with. It is better to take the time to line up the right people than to rush into a project with the wrong people. It will cost you significantly more in the long run if you have to find and pay someone else to fix mistakes.

Essential Criteria

There are four criteria you should keep in mind when vetting someone you will possibly work with. These criteria will help you choose someone that has the experience you are looking for, as well as a personality you can work with. It is important to choose people you feel you can work with. This is your project and you need to feel comfortable being direct and maintaining regular contact with people.

1. **Personal referrals.** Ask other people who have recently bought or sold a house, or had work done by a contractor, to see who they would or would not recommend. Ask people you trust to give you a clear and

honest answer. Just as you want to avoid people who would recommend anyone, you also want to avoid people that are overly negative about everyone.

2. **Solid references.** When you contact a professional, ask if she can provide you with references. If she has been in the business for any length of time, references shouldn't be a problem.

3. **Proven track record.** Ask them about their professional history. For a realtor, find out how many houses he has helped sell in the area you are thinking about working in. For financiers, ask them how many house flips they have been involved with. When talking to contractors, ask them if they have a portfolio for you to look at of past work.

4. **Personal impression.** Ask yourself how you felt talking to them. Did you feel like you were talking to someone you could trust, or did he leave you feeling like something was off about what he said? Did you get the clear impression that they are hard workers and take great pride in their work? If you don't feel right about a realtor, investor, or contractor, you don't need a concrete reason to not work with them. You can choose to trust your instincts.

ESSENTIAL

Think of references as personal referrals from people who haven't met you. Any professional should be able to provide you with the names of a couple people they've worked with in the past.

Interviewing Prospective Team Members

In order to discover how each professional stands up to your four criteria, you are going to need to talk to them all. While you don't have to call it an interview, you should go into the conversation with specific questions and goals in mind. This is your chance to get all the information you feel you will need to make the right decision. When setting the time for the meeting, let them know what you would like to see. For example, if you want to see a portfolio or plan to ask for references, you should let them know in advance, so they can be prepared for the meeting.

Making the Decisions

Once you talk to the professionals you are interested in working with, all that is left is to make a decision. Go back to your four criteria and consider your meeting. Choose your best candidates, and let them know you are interested in working with them. If there are other candidates that met your criteria, but weren't your first choice, let them know you will not need their services at this time, but you would like to hold onto their business card for possible future business. This will leave the door open in case your first choice doesn't work out.

Making Connections for Long-Term Benefits

Interviewing bankers and asking for referrals from realtors may seem extreme and it is probably unnecessary if you are only planning to flip one house and move on with your life. However, this is going to be a lot of work for a one-time experience. You need to go into this with the long-term in mind. There is a lot of money to be made in house flipping and you will gain a lot of personal freedom. Having the right people on your team will enable you to delegate more, micromanage less, and maximize the profits on every job.

Financial Benefits

In addition to making money flipping houses, developing professional relationships with the right people comes with financial benefits. Choosing the right realtor will enable you to get the best houses at the best prices and to sell houses quickly, so you can focus on the next project. Choosing the right financier or investor will ensure you have stress-free access to the money you need in order to complete the project fully and quickly.

In order to be successful at flipping houses, you need to be able to keep your end goal in mind at all times. Choosing the right professionals for your team may mean not choosing family and friends. Just because you are friends with someone does not mean they are good at their job and should be made a part of your professional team.

Choosing the right contractors will save you money, ensuring mistakes are not being made, which will allow you to maximize profits. Additionally, you can work out discounts with contractors for bulk work. Finally, contractors typically give preference to repeat customers when it comes to working projects into their timeline. Having a good relationship with your contractors can mean your projects will take priority.

Professional Connections

Developing these relationships also provides you with connections that can benefit you in the future. For example, instead of contacting your realtor when you're ready to buy a new house, your realtor may start contacting you when she finds a great deal that is probably going to move quickly. Likewise, when your supplier sees something going on clearance that you use on a regular basis, he may reach out to you before it is sold. These types of connections can help you grow your business quickly.

Real Estate Agents

Developing a relationship with a reliable real estate agent in your area can help you both buy and sell properties. A good real estate agent familiar with the area can alert you when good deals are coming onto the market. Agents can let you know when houses are going up for auction, bank owned, or at risk. They can help you connect with the people that are most interested in unloading the properties. For example, bank-owned properties are a great resource. Most banks are not interested in owning properties; they do so out of necessity. Therefore, they are generally eager to work with investors looking to buy bank-owned properties.

Having a real estate agent on your team can also help you sell properties quickly. Agents can help with your market research, and they can prepare marketing materials for you. They can put your property at the top of their show list when working with buyers. They can also help you connect with other property investors looking to buy.

How to Find the Right One

While you can start with referrals to find a realtor, a quicker method might be to check the local newspaper. See which realtors are mentioned multiple times in the paper with active listings and houses being sold in the area. This will show you which realtors know the area and are actively working the area you are interested in. Once you figure out who the most popular realtors are, you can set up meetings with them individually.

What Questions to Ask

One of the nice things about realtors is that every house they sell is essentially public record. If you doubt anything they're saying, you can easily verify the information. That being said, you want to ask them about their selling record: how many houses they have sold in your area of interest. Ask them the average time it takes them to sell a market-ready house. You should also ask them what kind of experience they have working with property investors, short sales, REO properties, etc. Because this is a somewhat specialized market, you want to work with someone who is already familiar with what you are trying to accomplish.

QUESTION

What if you find a realtor you really want to work with but he doesn't have experience with short sales, REO properties, etc.? Is it really that different?
A realtor that is eager and hard working can certainly learn quickly how to acquire properties through short sales, auctions, banks, etc. Everyone has to start somewhere. This will be a judgment call. If you find a realtor with the drive and work ethic, but not the experience, you can still choose to put him on your team.

Banks and Investors

Banks and investors can be difficult to develop a relationship with. Many people go into finding a bank with the idea that you just have to go with the bank that is willing to lend you the money. However, this is not the case. You need to choose a financier that you are comfortable working with. Even if the terms aren't exactly what you were hoping for, if you are comfortable with the arrangement, you can always work on better terms for future projects. Financiers tend to be overly cautious to protect their interests.

Banks

Start with the bank you already have a relationship with, wherever you've had an account the longest. Ask to talk to a loan specialist. Speak with the loan specialist about what you are planning to do to get a feel for how willing the bank is to work with property investors. You can also research which bank owns several of the properties you are interested in buying. They have a vested interest in selling the properties, so they may also be very willing to work with you.

When looking for a bank to work with, community banks and credit unions are also good places to check. Community banks and credit unions tend to be more invested in the local community. You are better able to talk to loan professionals about your particular needs as opposed to larger national banks, which are more likely to treat all loans the same regardless of who you are or your intentions.

Investors

Investors are completely different than banks. Investors are individuals or groups that are willing to invest their personal money into your project. Finding an investor means finding someone interested in taking the risk of investing. In order to develop a relationship with a potential investor, you need to be prepared to share your business plan and proposal for the properties you are interested in. You will also need to share your credentials in regard to the proposed business. An investor will be highly interested in what makes you qualified to successfully flip a house.

Working with a local investor will provide a better opportunity to develop an ongoing relationship. However, depending on the state you live in, there are also websites you can go to in order to find investors. These websites allow you to submit your business plan along with how much you need and what you're willing to give in return. People interested in investing read the profiles and decide who they want to invest in. These websites fall into the crowdfunding category; similar to the well-known Kickstarter.com (*www.kickstarter.com*), but tailored for equity investing. Fundrise.com and StartupValley.com are just two examples of the dozens of options for finding equity investors.

Contractors

You may need to work with a wide range of contractors since most contractors have specific specialties. Developing relationships with contractors that are reliable, fast, and affordable can help ensure that your projects get put to the top of the list, as the contractors work to make sure the project is done on time. Contractors are often eager to develop these relationships as well because it means long-term business for them. If a painter knows you'll hire her to paint every time you buy a property, she will make you a priority.

ESSENTIAL

Contractors often know other contractors. If you find one contractor you really like and want to work with, request his help in referring other contractors. As long as he is reputable, he won't knowingly refer another contractor that isn't reputable.

How to Find the Right One

When looking for contractors, referrals are often the best place to start. People who have actually hired contractors before will be able to tell you if they showed up when they said they would, finished the job when they said they would, and stayed within the estimated amount for the project. Personal referrals can also give you insight into the overall attitude and demeanor of the contractor and those that work for him or her. When looking for referrals, ask other property investors to see who they work with.

What Questions to Ask

When you meet with a potential contractor, ask to see pictures of some of their work. You may also be able to find pictures online before the meeting, if they have a business website. You should also ask contractors how long they've been in the business and how many crews they have working for them. This will give you insight into how large the company is, but also how much personal attention each project actually receives. Explain to them how important your timeline will be once you get started, and ask them if they will be able to commit to finishing the project as quickly as possible once they get started.

Supply Companies

The supply companies you work with will likely be big box stores like Lowe's or Home Depot, as well as some smaller stores for specialized products. For the big box stores, go visit their commercial sales desk. See about setting up a commercial account and talk to a commercial sales representative about their service and availability. You want to work with people who will return your phone calls in a reasonable amount of time.

When talking to smaller supply companies, you want to see exactly what they carry to make sure it is what you are interested in. You want to talk to the manager about their supplies, as well as their ordering system. You'll need to know if they bill or if they expect payment on delivery. Depending on what the product is, you will also need to know if they deliver and how much that costs per order. You can also ask if they offer business accounts. These accounts often streamline the ordering and payment process to make your job easier and with less paperwork. The commercial sales associate will also be able to help when you need to order additional supplies and have them delivered to the store.

Find the Best Suppliers for Your Needs

Unfortunately, in many areas, you may not have a lot of options in suppliers. You may have to work with a local supplier. Even if that is the case, attempting to establish a professional relationship with your local supplier can help you.

When you have options, you want to look for companies that can get you what you need at the best price. It is essential that they can accomplish both. Getting a great deal on something is useless if you can't actually get your hands on it for two months.

Working with Salespeople

Regardless of whether you are dealing with a commercial sales associate in a big store or the manager of a specialty supply store, you will be dealing with a salesperson. The goal of a salesperson is to make sales, and if you are talking to a good salesperson, you won't have to do too much to develop that relationship. A good salesperson will be eager to develop a relationship with you. However, you do want to be careful not to let yourself be talked into the upsells. A good salesperson will also always try to upsell you on the higher quality products or related products that you don't necessarily need. For example, you may be buying lumber, and the salesperson will try to sell you on the latest and greatest power tools. While these things may be tempting, you need to remember that every dollar you spend comes out of your profit. Know what you need before talking to your salesperson. This is the best way to make sure you aren't talked into buying things you don't really need.

FACT

Vendors and supply companies also participate in vendor and contractor shows. These are great events for networking, getting discounts on orders, as well as free samples of products. Let your commercial sales associate know you want to be put on the invite list for these types of events.

Inspectors and Appraisers

Developing relationships with both private and city inspectors will help you tremendously. Not that you can expect special treatment, but inspectors are just people like anyone else. If you get on their bad sides, you may encounter more red tape and hoops to jump through than others.

Appraisers are a little harder to develop a relationship with because you might not deal with the same appraiser twice. The best thing you can do is work on encouraging a positive experience while with an appraiser. If you work with this appraiser again, the positive spirit will already be there, and if you don't, you can at least make that one encounter go smoothly.

How to Foster a Positive Professional Relationship

The best way to get on an inspector's good side is by being polite, gracious, and showing you are putting forth honest effort. For example, if you did not realize something was not up to code, there are two ways you could choose to respond. The first way would be thanking the inspector for pointing that out and assuring him or her that you will address it immediately. Let the inspector know you did not realize it was not up to code, but you'll make sure you are on top of it on future projects. The second way you could deal with it would be cursing at the inspector and accusing them of not knowing what he is talking about or nitpicking to feel important. While this second option sounds ridiculous, people do it all the time. That is how you get on an inspector's bad side.

The same idea goes for appraisers. If you follow an appraiser around the property and nitpick everything she says about the house, you are going to annoy that person greatly, and that can impact their appraisal of the property. Although one could argue that personal feelings should have no affect on something like an appraisal, the fact of the matter is that it does. Appraisals, to an extent, are highly subjective. Once you get a bad appraisal, it will take multiple new appraisers and several lost days to prove the first appraisal to be inaccurate.

Avoiding Favoritism

It is important not to make your kindness come off as an attempt to sway an appraiser or inspector. This is especially true with city inspectors. While it would be completely normal to offer to buy one of your contractors lunch, you do not want to offer to buy lunch for the inspector. It is important that they don't appear to play favoritism, and that may be a concern if you try too hard. Keep everything very professional and focus on being receptive and polite.

City Officials

When it comes to getting permits, dealing with zoning issues, and more, having developed relationships with city officials is always beneficial. This isn't to say you'll get special treatment. However, you will have a better chance of not having to jump through extra hoops. Additionally, they may be more willing to work with you when there is a problem. For example, you may fill out the wrong paper or forget to sign something. Maintaining a positive relationship with the people accepting your paperwork or applications will encourage their assistance in making sure you have everything in order.

Who You're Really Dealing With

When it comes to dealing with city officials, it is important to know who you are really dealing with. In most cases, it is the gatekeepers that you need to develop good relationships with. These are the secretaries, receptionist, and assistants that take your applications, answer your phone calls, and decide who actually gets to talk to the official and who has to leave a message. Especially in larger areas, the actual city official in charge of issuing permits probably won't even see your application. They have people that sort through everything and issue the permits on their behalf.

ESSENTIAL

Dale Carnegie, an American writer and lecturer, once said, "There is nothing sweeter than the sound of one's own name." Learn the names of the people you are dealing with and use their names when you see them.

Fostering Positive Relations with City Officials

The best way to foster a positive relationship with the gatekeeper is to be polite and accommodating. They deal with plenty of rude, impatient, and annoying people. Working with someone who is friendly and polite will go a long way. When you're dropping something off, say hello, ask them about their day, and listen to their response. Don't just say, "How's your day? . . . I need to apply for a permit," and then hand them your paperwork. This tells them you don't really care, you're just going through the motions.

CHAPTER 5

Finding a Property

There are several qualities you want to look for in a property. First and foremost, you need to find a property that will allow you to make a profit. This means the gap between what the house is currently selling for and what it can sell for once it is renovated needs to be large enough that you can make all the needed renovations and still have plenty left over. The property also needs to be in the right neighborhood. You need to research your area to see where the best houses are for flipping. You want to find a house that has basic features that are sellable.

Choosing the Best Market for You

Choosing the best market is an essential part of finding a good property to flip. There are several market qualities you want to look for that a realtor can help you with. However, it is important to have a base of information. You will need to conduct research on an area in order to determine which market is best. Additionally, you need to decide what your market deal breakers are—the things that will make a certain area off limits to shop for properties.

Identifying Important Market Qualities

There are a few qualities to look for in a market. First, you will do best in a stable market. A buyer's market will allow you to buy a property cheaply, but it will also influence the selling price of the property. A seller's market means you're going to pay more for the property initially, but you'll also be able to sell it for more.

You want to find an area that does not have a glut of houses currently on the market. An area that is growing in population is ideal. The best market is one that is going through a revitalization. This often happens when new businesses are brought to an area and employment increases. More people are moving to the area, and the people already in the area might be looking to upgrade.

You also want to look for a market that is convenient. You'll need to travel there on a regular basis. You'll need easy access to resources like other professionals, contractors, suppliers for material needs, and more. Finally, it is always good to start with an area you are already familiar with. This will decrease the need to familiarize yourself with the area.

How to Effectively Research the Market

There are three effective ways to quickly research an area. First, read the paper. Look to see how many houses are selling and how many are for sale. Take note of the asking and selling prices. Look for information about new businesses opening up and new neighborhoods being built. Another feature to consider is the school system. Houses tend to sell better in areas with a good school system, especially if the area is surrounded by less than adequate school systems.

ESSENTIAL

Another great resource for market research is the National Association of Realtors (*www.realtor.org*). Without being a member, you can access their blog, podcasts, and a great deal of market research information through the organization's website.

The second place to do research is the County Auditor's website. This will provide more detailed information about houses being bought and sold in the area. It will also give you the tax value of the houses. While this is not the same as the appraised value, it is important to know, and it will provide insight into the property taxes. Prospective buyers will want to know what the property taxes are going to be.

Finally, work with a local realtor to learn more about the area. Make sure the realtor understands your goals and exactly what you are looking for. The realtor will also have better access to information on houses that are going through foreclosure or are already owned by the banks.

Deal Breakers

It is important to decide what qualities you will absolutely avoid. Two common deal breakers when choosing a house to flip are distance and comfort. Decide ahead of time how far you are willing to drive. You may decide you don't want to buy a house more than a twenty-minute drive from where you live. This will quickly narrow down the neighborhoods you are looking into. When determining driving distance, you also want to take into account where the supply stores are. You will likely be making regular runs to stores like Lowe's or Home Depot, so you want to know how far your supply stores are from the neighborhoods you are looking at.

The second common quality is comfort. You need to feel safe where you are working. So a deal breaker may be neighborhoods where you feel you wouldn't be safe working or visiting: day or evening. If a particular neighborhood has problems that concern you, you may also be at a greater risk of vandalism and theft during the project.

What to Look for in Your Search

Once you choose an area or two to look at, you can start looking for specific properties to buy. This is also an important process because the property you choose will directly impact the potential profit for the flip. Look at several potential properties in your chosen area. Looking at a lot of properties will give you a better overview of your options. Only looking at a couple properties is one of the most common mistakes new house flippers make.

Working with Your Realtor

Your realtor will be able to help you significantly in your house search. Your realtor will have access to listings of all the houses for sale in the area where you are looking. She will be able to arrange showings with private sellers and banks when necessary. Your realtor will most likely have contacts with inspectors, appraisers, and lenders.

Before you start your search, have a sit down with your realtor. Make sure the realtor knows exactly what you are looking for. Go over details like price, area, level of renovations needed, and the type of sale. For example, you may be only interested in bank-owned properties, so you don't need to work with private sellers. Or you may only be interested in properties with minimal renovations. These are all details you can go over with your realtor.

Making sure you and your realtor are on the same page will save you a significant amount of time. Once your realtor assembles a list of properties, you will need to go visit the properties to see if you are interested in buying them. You don't want to waste time looking at properties that aren't within your assigned parameters.

The Qualities You Want in a Property

Before going into your meeting with the realtor, it is best to start with a list of qualities you are looking for. This will ensure two things. First, it will ensure the realtor understands and remembers. You can give the realtor a copy of your list, so there is no confusion. Second, it will prevent you from forgetting to mention important criteria.

Here are a list of qualities to consider:

- Price range of house
- Type of sale
- Area where house is located
- Degree of renovations needed
- Age of the house

ALERT

Even if the price is right, avoid buying a "Franken-House." This is a term used to describe historic homes that have been added on to or partially renovated. These houses come with a whole host of renovation problems. Additionally, if it is a registered historic home, your hands will be tied by the local historical home association regarding what renovations you are even allowed to do.

Arranging Showings

There are two ways you can go about making a list of houses to see. First, you can trust your realtor to find only houses that fit your criteria. Your realtor will put together a list and set up showings for you to go to the properties. You can take a day or an afternoon going to each house on the list.

The second option is to have your realtor give you the list of addresses so you can do a couple quick drive-bys. You can go by the houses and create a short list of the few you are most interested in. As long as all the houses are relatively close together, so you aren't spending a lot of time driving, this method will save you a lot of time looking at houses.

Deal Breakers

Make a list of deal breakers, or things that will immediately eliminate a house from your consideration. In many situations, the price will be your primary deal breaker. However, you can choose other deal breakers, like renovations you don't want to deal with. For example, you may decide you don't want to renovate houses that have foundation issues that will need to be fixed. These types of problems can be big jobs that are both costly and time-consuming. Finding a house without a foundation issue will decrease the potential renovation projects to coordinate.

Assessing a Property

Part of choosing a property to buy will be assessing the property. When assessing a property as a potential flip, you will need to determine things like renovation costs and potential selling price, which will determine the potential profit. The higher the potential profit, the better. Assessing the potential in the property is also your opportunity to envision what the house can be. It takes a creative mind to see the potential beauty in houses that may be dirty and rundown.

Conducting an Inspection

Before buying a house, you will want to conduct an inspection of the house. This will enable you to come up with an estimation of the renovation costs. Knowing approximately how much the renovations will cost is essential to determining your potential profit.

You will need to inspect both the inside and the outside of the house. You will be looking for both major renovation needs, and minor or cosmetic needs. Major renovations would include changing the floor plan by adding a room or combining rooms, as well as things like replacing windows, the roof, the furnace, etc. Minor needs include things like replacing light fixtures, outlet covers, cabinet fronts, etc. Cosmetic needs often overlap with minor needs. They need to be done, but they have no structural impact on the house. For example, cosmetic renovations would include repainting, removing wallpaper, covering old paneling, replacing outdated fixtures, etc.

Estimating Renovation Costs

Once you have a list of the needed renovations, you can create an estimate for the renovation costs. To do this, you will need to go through your renovation list and assign an estimate cost to each item. Some costs will be more exact than others. For example, if you know the square footage of each room, you can estimate exactly how much paint you will need to repaint the interior of the house.

ESSENTIAL

Having a mentor in the house flipping business is a great way to ensure you are going about everything correctly. Estimating renovation costs is a good time to talk to your mentor before moving forward with the purchase.

For renovations that will require a professional, you can get a rough estimate from the contractor you will be working with. This will be a rough estimate because it will be based on the information you provide as opposed to the contractor actually going to the property and inspecting the renovation.

Once you have your list of estimated prices for each renovation, you can add them up to get a total estimate of renovation costs. You will then add that to the cost of acquiring the house. The total will be the total estimated expenses for the flip. You need to remember to figure in things like utility costs during the renovation, and rental costs for dumpsters or other needed equipment.

Determining Potential Selling Price

The selling price can be determined by looking at comparables in the area. Your realtor should be able to provide you with a list of comparables for houses that recently sold in the area, as well as houses that are currently for sale. For the houses that recently sold, look at both the asking price and the selling price to see how much the seller went down in order to make the sale happen.

Based on the information you collect about comparables, you will be able to determine what the approximate asking price will be for the renovated house. Your realtor can also supply you with an estimated asking price, but it is always best to do your homework to ensure the realtor is being realistic in their assumptions.

Determining Potential Profit

Once you have the estimated expenses and the approximate asking price, you can determine the potential profit. Subtract the total expenses from the estimated sale price of the house. Figure in the realtor fees and other closing costs. The amount you have left is the potential profit.

You want to have a goal profit in mind before going into a flip. This will help you decide if the house is going to be worth the effort renovating it. If you are particularly interested in a house, but the potential profit isn't as much as you were hoping for, you can look into ways to reduce the expenses. This can include negotiating down the selling price of the house. It can include reevaluating the list of renovations to see where you can save money. It can also include attempting to get a higher price for the house, but typically, the potential sale price of the house will be the most inflexible number you will be working with.

Home Inspections

Conducting an in-depth inspection of the property is an essential part of the process. The inspection allows you to fully understand exactly what needs to be done to the property. While there may be surprises after buying the house, most issues can be discovered during an inspection. The inspection allows you to make a list of needed renovations, estimate renovation costs, and create a realistic timeline for the renovation process.

QUESTION

What if you don't want to hire an inspector, and feel you are fully confident inspecting the house on your own?
Another option is to have a handyman or someone with renovating experience do the inspection with you. Although this person is not a trained inspector, he will have a good idea of what he is looking at and what kind of work is needed.

When You Can Only Conduct an Exterior Inspection

There are situations where you will be unable to conduct an interior inspection of the house. While this is not ideal, it doesn't have to automatically exclude a house from consideration. You can still conduct an exterior inspection, which will help you determine the status of the foundation, roof, windows, doors, exterior walls, and property. You can also look in the windows to get a small look at the interior's condition.

You can do some research to see how old the house is, how long it has been empty, and if there were any major renovations done prior to the house being abandoned. This type of information can provide significant insight into the potential renovations that may be needed.

Hiring an Inspector

If you do not have the time, know-how, or interest in inspecting the house yourself, you can also hire an inspector to do it for you. Talk to the inspector you choose, so he understands exactly what you are looking for. The cost associated with hiring an inspector will vary based on where you live. However, hiring an inspector will certainly save you on time.

Getting a Second Opinion

Whether you hire an inspector or do the inspection yourself, there may be situations where you want a second opinion from a specific professional. For example, if there is a concern about the foundation, you may want a professional contractor to come in and take a look at the foundation. Arranging this is generally as simple as setting up a second showing. When in doubt over a major renovation, it is always best to get a second opinion rather than just hoping for the best.

If arranging to have a contractor go to the house is not feasible, or you want to make an offer quickly, you can also take detailed pictures of the area you are concerned about and forward them to your contractor to look at. Your contractor should be able to give you an idea of what you are looking at and how bad it is based on the images.

Working with an Agent

It is not required that you work with an agent to look for properties. You can find all the information you need on your own, and you might think that this is an easy way to save money. However, when looking for properties, working with an agent is the easiest way to get the most information quickly. This is particularly true if you are new to the property market. Seasoned house flippers have a lot of their own contacts and access to information. However, they spent years building their resources of information.

Realtors are paid on commission, so it is in their best interest to work hard to help you accomplish your goals.

Benefits of Working with an Agent

A good realtor will be able to compile a list of prospects for you quickly. He will be able to make the needed arrangements for you to sell the properties, and he will effectively represent you to the seller regardless of whether it is a bank or private seller.

Working with a realtor will save you time, energy, and probably a good amount of frustration. Additionally, when working with realtors, they create and provide a lot of the needed marketing materials including taking pictures, making fliers, and advertising the house through local papers. This will save you time, money, and energy.

When to Look for a New Agent

Not all realtors are good realtors. Here are a list of situations where you need to consider finding a new realtor to work with:

- The realtor does not return your calls in a timely manner.
- The realtor takes you to see houses that clearly do not fit the criteria you provided.
- The realtor fails to effectively relay offer and counteroffer information.
- The realtor has no experience working with short sales, auctions, REOs, or pre-foreclosure sales.

When you decide you need to find a new realtor, it is best to break things off with the current realtor immediately, just so there are no misunderstandings. While this may be uncomfortable, it is simple. Call the realtor and say you've decided to go with another realtor. You can politely let the realtor know your exact reasons, or simply say for personal reasons. Keep in mind that this is your business, and you don't "owe" anyone, so do not let a realtor or anyone else try to pressure you or guilt you into working with them.

Buying "As-Is"

Buying "as-is" is when you agree to buy a house from a seller without any guarantees attached to the condition of the house. This allows you to buy a house without an official inspection. Buying "as-is" also means you have no recourse against the seller if the house requires more renovations than you originally expected. Oftentimes, houses being sold through a short sale, auction, or REO are only sold "as-is."

Advantages of Buying As-Is

The biggest advantage to buying a house "as-is" is that you can usually get a better price for the house. Accepting the financial responsibility of all renovations is an important aspect of the negotiations. Sellers can expect less when the house needs a lot of work. Agreeing to buy a house as-is will also give you greater access to houses that can be flipped for a good profit. There are many situations that can happen when dealing with banks when buying "as-is" is the only option.

Disadvantages of Buying As-Is

The greatest disadvantage of buying a house as-is is the risk involved. You are agreeing to accept whatever problems come with the house even if they turn out to be highly significant and more than you anticipated. However, this is the most basic risk of all house flipping. Being unwilling to take this risk means house flipping probably isn't for you.

How to Mitigate the Risks of Buying As-Is

You can mitigate risks by conducting a thorough inspection. The more you know about the house and its condition, the better prepared you will be going into the project. Additionally, if you know everything the house is going to need, you can make an educated decision regarding whether or not you should buy the house or look for a better option.

CHAPTER 6

Conducting an Exterior Inspection

Conducting an exterior inspection is an important step when deciding to purchase a property. Many flippers conduct their own inspections, rather than hiring an inspector to do it. Being able to conduct an inspection yourself will save you time and money, as well as provide you with a more solid understanding of the level of work needed to make the house sellable. If you do choose to hire an inspector, it is still essential for you to understand the types of damage you may be looking at. This chapter details the ins and outs of the inspection process, and will alert you to any potential damage in your property. Having this knowledge will enable you to make solid estimations when determining potential profit.

Preparing for an Exterior Inspection

If you feel you are able to conduct your own exterior inspection, and you are allowed to do so (i.e., you aren't buying a house as-is, or if the house isn't being foreclosed on), the next few sections will lead you through the process. Preparing to inspect the exterior of a property is fairly simple. While it may be intimidating if you've never conducted an inspection before, the following information will guide you through each step. The most important thing to remember is to make careful observations and write everything down. Even if you think you have a really good memory, you are going to be looking at a lot of things, and you'll need to remember many details about the house.

There are tools you will need to bring with you in order to conduct a thorough inspection. It is also important to have a procedure mentally prepared so you don't get overwhelmed once looking at the house. Following a procedure will ensure you inspect every aspect of the exterior.

Tools

There are a few tools you will need in order to do a complete exterior inspection. You will need:

- Flashlight
- Screwdriver
- Binoculars
- Level
- Six-foot ladder
- Notebook/notepad
- Pen
- Camera

These are the must-have tools. The flashlight will allow you to clearly see in dark or enclosed areas such as sheds, lofts in outbuildings, crawl spaces, under decks, and porches. You will need a screwdriver to test wood for rot or termite damage. The binoculars will allow you to examine the roof properly. The level will allow you to determine if all surfaces are flat, such as decks and porches.

The camera, notepad, and pen are needed so you can write detailed notes covering everything you discovered during the inspection. Taking pictures throughout your inspection in addition to the notes is also necessary. The pictures will help you better assess possible damage when reviewing your notes later. They will serve as reminders of things you noticed during the inspection, and they can be shown to contractors when getting estimates for work that needs to be done. Be sure to write the address of the house at the top of your notes and number the pages. This way if you inspect multiple houses or pages fall out of your notebook, you can still organize them.

In addition to these tools, you will need to wear work clothes, or clothes you won't mind getting dirty. You will likely be going into dirty areas or needing to get down on the ground in order to inspect everything. You need to go into the inspection prepared to get messy. You also need to be prepared mentally that you may run into insect infestations, animal infestations, as well as potentially disgusting situations. Oftentimes, when a house has been abandoned, things were not left in good condition, the house may have been vandalized while empty, or the mere lack of attention has resulted in decay and infestation.

The Top-Down Exterior Inspection Process

When conducting an exterior inspection, you want to work from the top down. This means start by inspecting the roof and work your way down to the foundation. This will help you stay mentally organized and keep your notes organized. Having a set procedure you follow will also help prevent you from missing issues with the house.

As you are doing the inspection, you will be making several trips around the house. As you do more inspections and get more comfortable, you can consolidate your passes. For example, when first starting out, you should do one pass just to inspect the exterior walls and another pass to inspect the exterior of the windows. However, as you get more proficient, you can inspect both the walls and windows in the same pass.

Taking your time, especially in the beginning, is essential. With this in mind, be prepared to let the realtor or homeowners, if they are still in the house, know you will be there for a while doing the inspection. It is important not to let people rush you through the inspection; this may cause you to miss major problems with the property.

Roof

There are two basic categories of roofs: pitched roofs and flat roofs. For each type of roof, there are different types of covers used to protect the house from the elements. Overall, there are a few things you need to look for aside from the type of covering used. For example, a pitched roof has two basic components: the deck and the covering. The deck is the actual surface of the roof. The covering is what protects the deck from the weather.

For both pitched roofs and flat roofs, proper ventilation directly below the deck is essential. Make sure to check the ventilation while inspecting the roof and while inspecting the attic. Lack of ventilation below the roof can lead to a number of problems.

Pitched Roofs

When inspecting a pitched roof, the first thing you want to do is back away as far from the house as you can and look at the roof as a whole. Visually look at each portion or slope of the roof. You are looking for sagging, damaged, obviously repaired, or uneven areas. Sagging and uneven areas are indications that there may be damage to the roof deck. You also want to make a note if there are any portions of the covering missing or clearly damaged. The deck in damaged areas will need inspection, and the covering will need to be replaced.

Take note of whether the roof is going to need to be cleaned. Sometimes you will see roofs that appear black in areas. This does not necessarily mean the covering is bad or needs replacement. For a couple hundred dollars, you can have a roof bleach-cleaned, which will make it look fresh and new. You also want to look for any structures that may need further inspection. Make note of chimneys, vents, skylights, etc. Finally, look around the entire house to see if there are any trees or low-hanging limbs that may cause a problem in the near future.

There are a wide variety of things you need to look for depending on the type of roof and covering you are inspecting. It is important to take detailed notes and take pictures to accompany those notes. This will allow you to go to a roofing professional and get a reliable estimate on potential repair costs if there are issues. Roof repairs can get expensive fast, so it is important to get an accurate understanding of the roof's condition prior to purchasing a property.

Shingles

Shingles are a type of roof covering commonly used on residential homes. There are several types of shingles to be aware of because they each come with their own unique problems. There are asphalt shingles, wood shingles, asbestos-cement shingles, slate shingles, metal shingles, and clay tiles. Regardless of the type of shingles, if you discover the roof has been recently repaired or re-shingled, find out when and if there is a warranty. Getting a copy of any warranty paperwork is important because it can allow you to avoid an unneeded expense. If repairs need to be made while still under the warranty, with the paperwork in hand, you won't have to worry about paying for them.

Asphalt Shingles

If the house has asphalt shingles, you need to look for shingles that are missing, cracked, curling, or otherwise damaged. You can replace areas of shingles without re-shingling the entire roof. If there is a buildup of what looks like gravel on the roof, that is a sign that the shingles are deteriorating. Work with the realtor or previous owners to determine how old the shingles are and how many layers of shingles are on the roof. Oftentimes, when new shingles are needed they are installed right on top of the old shingles to save time and money, but this can create its own set of problems.

Wood Shingles

If the house has wood shingles, look for shingles that are missing, cracked, loose, or otherwise damaged. Similarly to asphalt shingles, you can replace individual shingles if the majority of the shingles are in good condition. With wood shingles, it is also important to look for signs of rot. This is especially important for any areas of the roof that are well shaded by trees. Since shaded areas are more likely to hold moisture longer, they may rot faster than the areas getting full sun. Look for moss growth on the roof. If moss is present, those areas will need further inspection for rot.

Slate or Asbestos-Cement Shingles

If the house has slate or asbestos-cement shingles, you want to look for shingles that are missing, chipped, cracked, or loose. Slate and asbestos-cement shingles will naturally last significantly longer than other types of shingles. However, they are more brittle and therefore more prone to cracking or chipping. If well-maintained, slate shingles can last for well over 100 years. You also need to inspect the nails. Look for nails that are missing or appear to be rusting. On really old houses, it is not uncommon for nails to rust away. This creates the potential for water leakage, and a higher risk of shingles coming loose or falling off during a storm.

Clay Tiles

Similarly to slate and asbestos-cement shingles, clay tiles can last a really long time. However, they are the easiest to break. So you want to pay special attention for broken, chipped, and cracked tiles that will need to be replaced. Check the valley joints between the slopes to see if they are filled with asphalt cement. Also check for snow guards along the lower edge of roof tiles. These should be in place to protect the lower levels from breaking under the weight of the snow.

Metal Shingles

Metal shingles or panels are significantly less likely to be damaged than slate shingles or clay tiles. However, that does not mean the roof will not be an issue for you. You need to inspect the roof, looking for loose nails and loose panels. You also need to inspect the shingles to see if any are dented or faded. You need to check the joints and valley sections to see if they are covered with roofing cement.

FACT

Metal roofs reflect 70 percent of the sun's energy away from the structure, making them more energy efficient than other roofing options. According to research conducted by the Florida Solar Energy Center, structures with metal roofs experience 34 percent less heat gain than structures with asphalt shingles.

Flat Roof

A flat roof will need to be inspected from the rooftop. While pitched roofs are designed to get rain and snow to slide down off the roof, flat roofs drain precipitation, so it is essential that they have watertight sealing to protect the roof while the water is draining.

The first thing you need to inspect is the roof access. There needs to be safe and easy access to the roof. Once on the roof, you need to walk the entire roof looking for cracks, blisters, erosion, punctures, and torn or split covering. Any damage to the roof covering can result in interior water damage, which you will need to look for during the interior inspection. In addition to potential water damage, the roof will need to be repaired.

You also need to check all the joints and seams to make sure there are no breaks or gaps where water could be getting through. You need to check the roof drainage to make sure it is adequate and fully functional. Look around for accumulating water. It is best, if possible, to inspect a flat roof after it has rained. This will allow you to see if there is an excessive puddle situation.

Rooftop Structures

While inspecting the roof, it is also important to inspect all rooftop structures. This may include roof vents, vent stacks, hatches, skylights, chimneys, gutters, and downspouts. While the gutters and downspouts aren't exactly rooftop structures, they are essential to the condition and maintenance of the house. It is easiest to inspect them during this portion of the inspection.

For roof vents, stacks, and skylights, the concerns are basically all the same. You need to check all the joints to make sure they are properly covered. Look for gaps, cracking, or deteriorating material. Joints are potential weaknesses in the roof, and leaks often start here. Check the tightness of joints during the roof inspection, and you'll want to check them again while inspecting the attic. Additionally, for skylights, you want to make sure none of the panels are cracked or loose, and the window frame is in good condition.

Chimneys

There are two types of chimneys that may be present: masonry chimneys and metal chimneys. Masonry chimneys need to be inspected for sections that may be cracked, loose, eroded, or crumbling. Check both the bricks and the mortar for weaknesses and damage. Check the joints to make sure there are no cracks, gaps, deterioration, or other types of damage. Make sure the chimney is vertical and not leaning. If the house has a flat roof, the chimney needs to be at least three feet above the roofline. Inspect the chimney flashing for damage, and if possible, check to see if the flue is lined. You also want to check for a damper. If it is a metal chimney, you want to look for holes, rust, missing sections, or noticeable damage. You also want to make sure there is a rain cover present.

Gutters and Downspouts

There are two basic types of gutters you may encounter: exterior-mounted gutters and built-in gutters. For built-in gutters, you want to check for signs of leakage or seepage below the gutters. As part of this inspection, you want to look for areas of rotting trim. Rotting trim will need to be replaced, but this is also a sign that the gutters are leaking and will need to be repaired or replaced.

ESSENTIAL

A gutter strap is a metal band that is used to support the weight of the gutter. Gutters that are sagging or pulling away from the house are likely to have loose or missing gutter straps. Replacing or tightening gutter straps is a relatively simple and inexpensive job.

For exterior-mounted gutters, you want to start by writing down the type of material used. They may be aluminum, galvanized iron, wood, or copper.

The material used will significantly influence repair and replacement costs, so it is important to note. You then want to look for sections of gutter that might be missing, hanging from the house, or pulling away from the house. For metal gutters, you want to look for holes, sagging, visible signs of leakage, and loose or missing gutter straps.

For wood gutters, you want to look for visible signs of leakage and cracked or rotting gutters. If you aren't sure if an area is rotting, you can poke at it with the screwdriver you brought. Rotting wood will be spongy and easy to pierce and break away with a screwdriver.

While the downspouts should be the same material as the gutters, you want to take note of any differences. Then check for missing and damaged downspouts. Check all the joints where the downspouts are attached to the gutters to make sure they are secure and not leaking. Check for holes, missing elbows, loose or missing straps, broken or gapping seams. Any damage in the downspouts can result in water buildup near the foundation, which can cause damage to the foundation and increase the risk of water in the lower level of the house. At the end of the downspouts, check to make sure the water is being directed away from the house with the use of extensions, elbows, and splash plates. Check for areas where water is puddling up against the foundation of the house.

Garage

There are two basic types of garages: attached and detached. While the size of the garage does not matter in regard to the inspection, you should write down the size of the garage because it may be an important point for determining repair costs and resale value. The inspections for these two types of garages will be different because they each come with their own concerns.

Attached Garage

First, make sure the door going from the garage to the house is at least one step up from the garage floor. This door should be an exterior door with a strong seal to protect the house from garage fumes. The side of the door facing the garage should be metal. The garage should be built on a raised slab. These are all safety concerns and should be checked first. While all these features should be there, garages built by nonprofessionals or without proper inspection may have been built wrong.

Check the garage ceiling for stains or patches that may indicate water damage. Check the floor for cracks or missing sections. Make sure the floor is even. Make sure the driveway is not inclined toward the garage. Check the main exterior door for damage. Make sure it opens and closes easily and can be locked. Check overhead garage doors to make sure they are fully functional. Check the overhead doors for damage, cracks, peeling, signs of rot, or insect damage. If the overhead door is electric, make sure the door stops and goes up, and note if it hits something. Check the garage lights to make sure they are operational. Check any windows for damage. Make sure all the windows open and close properly. Check the window panels to make sure none of them are loose or damaged.

Detached Garage

Start with the exterior of the garage. Walk around the entire garage twice, making notes of what you see. Write down the material used for the exterior walls. Check for missing, loose, cracked, damaged, or rotting sections of the wall. Check all the windows for missing, cracked, loose, or broken glass panels. Check the window frames for damage, rot, or gapping.

Check the roof for sagging or damaged areas. Check for signs of rot, especially in shaded areas. Inspect the roof shingles for damaged, missing, chipped, broken, or deteriorating shingles. Check the gutters and downspouts; looking for missing, hanging, loose, or damaged sections. Check for missing or loose hardware. Make sure the water is being directed away from the garage.

Go around the garage with your screwdriver and check the trim around the doors and windows for rot, swelling, or bulging areas. Check the outside of the overhead garage door. Make notes if it is cracked, damaged, splintered, or otherwise damaged. Make sure the door works properly. Check the main door for damage and make sure it works properly.

Interior Concerns

Once inside the garage, check the ceiling for signs of damage or leakage. Check the floor for cracks, erosion, missing sections, or uneven settling.

Write down the material of the floor. Check the interior walls and window sills for damage, rot, and signs of insect infestation.

Make sure the garage is properly vented. If there is electricity in the garage, make sure it is installed and working properly. Check for inadequate or makeshift wiring. If the garage is heated with a space heater, make sure the heater is functioning properly and positioned safely. Generally speaking, there is a greater chance of makeshift work in detached garages than attached garages, so it is important to make sure everything is installed properly and up to code.

ESSENTIAL

Adding electricity to a detached garage or structure is a relatively simple task and will increase the perceived value of the property. However, it is a task that should be reserved for a professional. The electric codes for running electricity to an unfinished structure are different than finished structures.

Exterior Paved Areas

Exterior paved areas include the driveway, the sidewalk (if there is one), and any paved walkways around the house. If there is an in-ground pool, this may also include the cement pad or walkway around the pool. While it is not necessarily essential to repair minor damage to paved walkways, you want to look for areas that are unsafe, can cause drainage issues, or areas that may be signs of other problems.

Sidewalks

Check all sidewalks and paved pathways around the house, leading up to the house, and at driveway level. Look for areas that are cracked, missing, chipped, broken, eroded, or uneven. You need to determine if any section of the sidewalk creates a significant tripping hazard. Check the sidewalks around the house to see if any of them are pitched toward the house causing water to puddle along the foundation. You also want to look for trees along any walkways that may cause damage in the foreseeable future.

Driveway

Driveways should be 8 to 9 feet wide for a single vehicle. While this may be assumed, double check to make sure. Walk the entire driveway, looking for areas that are cracked, eroded, settled, and visibly damaged. Take pictures to record the extent of the damage. Check for uneven areas where water may be puddling. Make sure there is adequate drainage for water runoff. Damage to paved areas can usually be repaired without having to replace the entire area.

Outdoor Structures

Outdoor structures may include a deck, patio, porch, fences, barn, shed, or other type of structure. The number of outdoor structures will vary from one house to the next. Generally speaking, outdoor structures that are usable and in good condition will increase the value of the property. Homeowners like having the availability of these extra features. However, if the outdoor structures are going to cost thousands in repairs to make them usable, they will hurt the property's overall potential for profit.

Decks, Patios, and Porches

For decks, patios, and porches, the inspection needs will depend on the material used, the size, and whether or not it is attached to the house. Be sure to record the material used in your notes for future reference.

For stone or cement decks or patios, look for cracked, chipped, uneven, or visibly damaged areas. Be sure to take pictures of the damage, if present. If the patio, deck, or porch is wood, check for signs of rot or insect damage. Check for cracked, splintered, uneven, or otherwise damaged boards. Check all joints for gapping. If the structure is attached to the house, check to see if it is attached with lag bolts or just nails. It should be attached with lag bolts. A lag bolt is a heavy-duty wood screw. It will have a square or hexagon-shaped head that requires a wrench to adjust. These are significantly stronger than regular nails or screws and should be used when attaching decks.

If the structure is not built on the ground, check the support system under the structure. Make sure the support is adequate for the size of the structure, and there are no signs of damage. If there is wood support, check for signs of rot or insect damage. Check steps and rails for sections that are damaged, missing, or insecure. If the structure is painted, take note of flaking or discolored areas that will need to be repainted. If there is lighting, check to make sure it is operational.

Fences

Note the material used to make the fence: wood, metal, and composite are the most common. For wood fences, walk the entire fence looking for missing, loose, cracked, or damaged sections, as well as signs of rot or insect damage. For metal fences, walk the entire fence looking for areas that are missing, loose, damaged, rusted, bent, or disfigured. For composite fences, check for sections that are missing, loose, or discolored. Regardless of the fence material, check all gates. Check for missing or broken hardware. Open and close the gate to make sure it opens and closes evenly. Make sure the latch is secure and the gate stays level while in the open position.

FACT

Many communities have regulations regarding the types of fences you can have, how high the fence can be, and where fences can be installed. Check with local laws and regulations before spending the time and money to repair an existing fence or install a new one.

Barns and Sheds

Record the building material used. The exact inspection needs will vary depending on the material used, the size of the structure, and how finished it is. For example, a premade metal shed without electricity will require far less inspection than a fully operational wood barn with water and electricity.

When inspecting an outdoor structure, focus on looking for any kinds of damage. If there are utilities running to the building, check to make sure they are properly installed, working, and safe. Check the roof, walls, foundation, drainage, and condition just as you would other areas of the house.

Pool

Pools can be a major selling point for potential buyers or a huge hassle. Your pool inspection is essential in determining the future of the pool at your property. In some situations it will be more timely and cost-effective to eliminate the pool than to get it in sellable condition. Do not assume the presence of a pool will increase your potential profits. The first thing you want to check is if the pool has a fence that encloses the entire pool and if the fence gates are self-closing and self-latching.

ALERT

Having a secure fence is particularly important if there is an in-ground pool. In many areas, fencing around an in-ground pool is a legal requirement, so it is important to check local laws on this matter. Additionally, insurance companies generally require a fence for an in-ground pool in order for the buyer to get homeowners insurance.

There are two basic types of pools: concrete pools and vinyl-lined pools. If it is a vinyl-lined pool, you want to check the vinyl to see if it is stained, discolored, or torn in any areas. You also want to make sure the liner is securely attached in all areas, not pulling away from the edge or about to pull loose.

If the pool is concrete, check the tiles to see if any area is missing, loose, cracked, chipped, or otherwise damaged. Check to see if any of the tiles or plaster are discolored or flaking. If there are painted areas, check to see if any of the paint is faded or flaking. Check the condition of both the strainer basket and skimmer weir.

If there is a pool deck, you will need to inspect that for areas that are cracked, chipped, splintering, uneven, or otherwise damaged. Check the ladder and rails to make sure they are all steady and sufficiently anchored. If there is a slide or diving board, check to make sure they are properly anchored. You also want to check slides and diving boards for cracks, chips, or warped and uneven areas.

You also need to check the pump, filtration system, heater, and any other pool equipment to make sure they are fully operational. Check for rust or scale buildup, water puddling, or dripping around the pump and heater. If there are underwater pool lights, make sure they are all operational and in good condition. If there is a pool cover, make sure it isn't ripped or visibly damaged. These are all things that can be replaced, if needed. When doing your research on the area, check to see the difference in selling price between properties with and without a pool. If the cost of repairing the pool exceeds the potential profit in having a pool, the best decision is to get rid of the pool.

Landscape

When looking at the landscape, you need to think practically and aesthetically. The front landscape is one of the first things prospective buyers are going to see when coming to the property. An inspection of the landscape needs to include an inspection of the drainage, lawn, shrubs, and trees.

Drainage

First, check to see if the house is located in a flood plain. Even if the house is not in an official flood plain, check to see if there are flooding risks such as nearby creeks or streams. Check to see if the property is level or inclined, and if it is inclined toward or away from the house. Check to see if the street is inclined and where the house is located on the street in regard to the incline. Check into the street drainage to see if it is present and how efficient it is. Look at the neighbors on either side to see if their properties are flat or sloped, and if they are sloped toward or away from your property. Any incline toward the house can increase the potential risk of flooding in the house.

QUESTION

What can be done if there are flooding risk factors, but the property is otherwise ideal?
While you cannot easily change the topography of the land, you can install or upgrade the drainage system. The cost of repairing or upgrading a drainage system will vary greatly depending on the size of the property and the condition of the current system. However, homeowners pay an average of $1,200–$2,000 when repairing their drainage system.

Check to see if there are low areas on the property that may be more prone to collecting and holding water. Although you shouldn't exclusively make a decision based on what others say, don't be afraid to ask the neighbors about the drainage. Ask them if the yards tend to flood when it rains and how quickly the water goes away.

Lawn and Shrubs

Walk around the lawn looking for holes or sunken areas. These could be signs of animal issues. Survey the yard for areas of dead or lack of grass that may need to be reseeded. Survey the shrubs to determine if there is overcrowding, dead or dying shrubs, blocked walkways, or vine plants near the house. While they look nice, vines can be highly destructive to a house. Take pictures of shrubs you think will need removal, transplanting, or pruning. In most cases, landscape issues cost more time than money to fix.

Trees

Check all the trees on the property for signs of rot or insect infestation. Look for dead trees or limbs that will need removal. Check for trees or limbs that are hanging over the house, outdoor structures, or electrical wires that may need trimming or removal. Often when a tree is rotting, it starts on the inside, which makes it harder to detect. Hit several areas in the tree's trunk with a rubber mallet to see if any areas sound hallow. Also, look for holes or crevasses forming in the tree's trunk. Excessive growth of fungi or ferns on the base of the tree can also be signs of rot; these plants feed on rotting wood.

Take note of trees that are grossly overgrown or in a bad location. Also take note of the types of trees on the property. You'll want to know if the trees on the property are flowering, fruit bearing, or produce anything that could be considered advantageous or displeasing. For example, if there are three healthy apple trees on the property, you can use that as a selling point for potential buyers.

Exterior Doors and Windows

Exterior doors and windows will need to be inspected during both the interior and exterior inspection of the house. Doors and windows are very significant because they affect the house and its value in so many ways. Doors and windows need to provide aesthetic value, protection, usability, as they greatly influence the energy efficiency of the house, by determining both the amount of natural light and the house's ability to maintain temperature.

Windows

Note whether the windows are wood or vinyl. If possible, find out the age of the windows and if any have recently been replaced. If there were windows recently replaced or installed, try to find out if there is any kind of warranty on the new windows. Older wood, single-panel windows are highly energy inefficient. If these are present in the house, you need to consider the cost of all new windows.

Check all the panels in all the windows to see if any are cracked, broken, or missing. Make sure each pane is properly secured to the sashes. Look at the window for signs of rot or damage. Take note of whether or not they are painted and if the paint is chipped, flaking, or noticeably faded. If the windows have been painted at any time, check to see if any of them have been painted shut.

Doors

Check each exterior door and write down the material of the door and the age, if you know it. Make sure all the doors can be securely locked. If the doors have windows in them, check the window panes to see if any are cracked, broken, missing, or loose. If the door is wood, look for cracks, chips, or other damage. Check to see if the door is warped. If the door is fiberglass, look for cracks in the door. If the door is metal, check for noticeable dents or scratches. Finally, check the weather-stripping around the exterior joints of the door to make sure it is present and adequate.

Walls

Similar to the roof, there are a variety of materials that may be used for the exterior covering of the walls. The possible materials include wood, aluminum siding, vinyl siding, stucco, and masonry. The cost of repairs will be determined by the material used and the extent of the damage.

Wood Siding

There are multiple types of possible wood exteriors. These include siding, shingles, plywood panels, and boards. Walk around the entire house looking for missing, broken, loose, cracked, or split wood. Check for signs of rot or discoloration. Check wood for warped areas. If the wood is painted, check for peeling or flaking paint. If the exterior is wood boards, check for loose or missing knots, cracked or blistering sections, and open joints. For plywood panels, check for open or gapping joints, warped panels, and loose, cracked, or otherwise damaged sections. Finally, check the bottom of the wall to make sure the wood stops at least 8 inches above the ground. Damaged areas in wood exteriors can generally be repaired or replaced without having to redo the entire exterior.

Aluminum and Vinyl Siding

Check siding joints to make sure they are weather tight. Check for an insulation backer under the siding. For aluminum siding, check for dented, loose, missing, or otherwise damaged areas. For vinyl siding, check for blistered, wavy, sagging, loose, missing, cracked, or otherwise damaged areas. If the siding has been painted, check for chipping, flaking, or noticeably fading paint. If there is unpainted vinyl, it is considered maintenance-free, so you just need to check for damaged areas. Do not paint vinyl siding if it is not already painted; this will create a future maintenance issue for the homeowner.

Stucco

Stucco is a combination of cement, sand, water, and lime applied in layers. Typically, it is applied in two layers when going over masonry and three layers when going over wood. Stucco is beneficial because it is resistant to termites, rot, and it is naturally weather-resistant. It is also very hard and durable. While this is beneficial in most situations, settling can cause the stucco to crack. Once cracked, it can be compromised by water damage. All cracks, regardless of their size and depth, need to be sealed.

When inspecting a stucco house, it is important to walk around the entire house looking for cracks, chips, bulging, or damaged sections. Make note of the damaged areas and take pictures of the damage to determine severity and degree of work needed to repair. If the house is painted, check the paint for chipping or flaking.

Masonry

Masonry walls may be comprised of clay tile, concrete block, brick, or stone. Masonry walls are generally more expensive to install and repair. However, they are more energy efficient, more durable, and will last longer than other types of exterior walls. Additionally, masonry walls provide the support and the covering all in one. Other types of exterior walls are coverings installed over wood frames.

Inspect the entire exterior of the house looking for areas with loose or bulging masonry. Look for deep cracks around the doors and windows. Check for cracked, missing, or otherwise damaged stone or bricks. Check mortar for missing, loose, cracked, or deteriorating sections. Missing, broken, and damaged bricks or stones will need to be replaced. Damaged mortar can be repaired fairly easily.

Energy Considerations

With the rising cost of utilities and an overall increase in environmental concerns, energy considerations are important when trying to sell a house. With that in mind, you can check for energy-saving features while conducting your exterior inspection.

Doors and Windows

If the house has single-pane windows, check to see if it comes with storm windows. If so, see if there are storm windows for all the windows in the house. If they are not on the house, ask to see them. Check for missing, cracked, and broken panes. Make sure the frames aren't bent and all necessary hardware is present. Likewise, check to see if the house has a storm door. If it does, check the quality of the door. Make sure it is operational and has the necessary hardware. Check all the doors and windows for weather-stripping, and make sure all the joints are properly sealed. Check all caulk to see if it is peeling, cracked, missing, or otherwise damaged.

If the windows or doors are really old or in really bad condition, you may need to replace them. While this may be a significant expense, new energy-efficient doors and windows are a great selling point. If you don't want to replace all the doors or windows, installing new weather stripping and re-caulking all the joints can go a long way in helping to stabilize the interior temperature of the house.

CHAPTER 7

Conducting an Interior Inspection

When conducting an interior inspection, you need to determine what items need to be replaced, repaired, or just need to be cleaned. Taking notes and pictures as you go through the house will better enable you to estimate renovation costs and time, as well as the potential profit. In most cases, many of the needed repairs are cosmetic improvements, which will increase the perceived value and enable you to sell the house faster and for more money.

Preparing for an Interior Inspection

When preparing to conduct an interior inspection, you need to be both physically and mentally prepared. Physically, you need to have the proper tools ready. You need to have plenty of time to fully inspect the house, and you need to be wearing work clothes, as you can get dirty checking attics, basements, and crawl spaces. Mentally, you need to be prepared for whatever is in the house. When houses are abandoned, the house is often found full of trash, the previous resident's possessions, and more. House flippers have gone into houses to find food still in the fridge rotting away, animals living in the house, and bathrooms that were still used after the utilities had been shut off in the house. While not all houses are left in disgusting conditions, many are.

Tools

The interior inspection will utilize many of the same tools as your exterior inspection. For an interior inspection, you will need:

- Electric tester
- Level
- Flashlight
- Screwdriver
- Notebook/notepad
- Pen
- Camera
- Six-foot ladder

FACT

You may be tempted to buy a thermal tester to inspect for energy losses in and around the house. However, these are not always accurate and even less accurate when not operated by a professional. Save your money and just inspect the windows and doors.

These are the most basic tools you will likely need to conduct your inspection. If the electricity to the house has been turned off, you won't be able to check the outlets to see if they work, so the electric tester will be dependent on the situation. The level will allow you to determine if floors, shelves, and counters are level. The flashlight will allow you to see in dark and dingy areas of the house. The screwdriver will enable you to check for rotting wood. The notebook and pen are so you can take notes during the inspection, and the camera can help you visually record damage you want to look at again later.

Process

With the interior inspection, you want to start at the top and work your way down. This means two things. First, you want to start at the top of the house, so that means starting with the attic and working your way down to the basement. Obviously, if you are inspecting a house that doesn't have an attic or basement, you just work your way from the highest point of the house to the lowest point of the house.

This also means that in each room, you want to work from the ceiling down. Following this procedure in every room will ensure you inspect everything and you stay organized throughout your inspection. You want to make sure you inspect every room, which includes closets and storage areas.

Windows and Doors

Inspecting doors and windows as part of an interior inspection is very important. This part of the inspection will include inspecting the interior of the windows, the interior side of the exterior doors, and all the interior doors. Doors and windows represent a significant possible expense while renovating, so be diligent and thorough.

Windows

Replacing windows can get very expensive very quickly depending on the number of windows you need replaced. Even if the windows look bad, really take the time to inspect them. Finding out that they can be fixed or even just cleaned will save a lot of money in total renovation costs. Common and easily fixable problems with windows include cracked or chipped panes, windows being painted shut, missing hardware, or windows not opening and closing easily.

When inspecting the windows, you first want to open and close each window to make sure it works properly. Check for cracked or broken window panes that will need to be replaced. While checking the panes, also check for missing putty, as that will also need repair. If there are wood window sills, take note of their condition; both structurally and aesthetically. If the windows were leaking at any point, a wood window sill can rot. Check for rot by carefully prodding the edges of the window sill with the screwdriver. Rotting wood will easily break away.

For double hung windows, check the sash cords to see if they are missing or broken. You also want to check for loose or binding sashes. For thermal-pane windows, check for signs of moisture between the panes. This may include fogginess or water condensation on the inside of the glass. For steel-casement windows, check for rusting or strung frames. You also want to see if the windows have or come with screens and the condition of the screens. Broken screens can easily be fixed if the frames are in good condition.

Doors

When checking the interior of exterior doors, check to make sure the door locks properly. Check the door itself to make sure it is solid, secure, and in good condition, and if the weather stripping needs to be replaced. Take note of the interior of the door and whether it will need to be repainted. Check the door knob and hinges to make sure they are all in good condition.

ALERT

Be sure to check behind all the interior doors to make sure there isn't a hole where the doorknob might have hit the wall. Walking into a room, people often forget to close the door from the inside and check behind it.

Next, look at all the interior doors to make sure they are in good condition. Check the doors for cracks, holes, splintering wood, and missing or broken hardware. Make sure they open and close properly. If the doors have locks, make sure they lock and unlock properly. Make sure, at the very least, the bathroom doors have locking doors. Keep in mind that the more repairs the house needs, the more money it will cost. The inspection is your chance to see if the house is financially a good option for a flip.

Walls, Ceilings, and Floors

When inspecting the walls, ceilings, and floors, you need to check them for function, structure, and aesthetics. Walls, ceilings, and floors that are cracked or bowed may have water or structural damage. In terms of aesthetics, you need to check the coverings. For example, the kitchen floor may be in great shape structurally, but it is covered with disgusting, ugly, and cracked tile. This means you are going to have to replace the floor covering. In each room, start with the ceiling, then go to the walls, and finally the floor. If there is damage to the floor on an upper level, be sure to closely inspect the ceiling of the room below the damaged area.

Ceilings

Check the ceilings for water stains, cracks, and holes. Check to see if the ceiling appears to be peeling or collapsing in any areas. If an area looks different or recently repaired, touch the ceiling in that area to see if it feels spongy. This can be an indication of water damage. Take note if the ceilings are going to need repainting.

If there are drop ceilings in any of the rooms, check above the drop ceiling to see the condition of the real ceiling. Drop ceilings are often used to cover up ceiling damage or other issues. They are most common in the kitchen area, but may be used throughout a house.

Walls

When it comes to interior walls, you have to assume you'll need to repaint inside. A fresh coat of paint will give everything that new clean look and feel when showing the house to prospective buyers. With that in mind, don't worry too much about the condition of the paint. When inspecting interior walls, you want to look mostly for damage. Water damage and structural issues are big expenses, so those are your primary concerns.

Look for cracks or holes in the walls, as well as for bulging, blistered, or otherwise damaged areas. Look for water stains on the ceilings and walls. Look for missing, sagging, broken, or loose ceiling tiles. Check all installed ceiling fans and lights to see if they work. Check for cracks where the walls meet the ceiling.

If the windows and doors are not level or won't open properly, look closely for any cracks in the walls. These can indicate structural problems. Check all the interior trim for missing, loose, or broken pieces. If there is paneling on any of the walls inside the house, be aware that the condition of the walls under the paneling may be questionable. While paneling did go through a period of popularity, it was also commonly used to cover up damaged walls.

ESSENTIAL

If you are unsure about the condition of a wall behind paneling, it might be best to leave the paneling. You can easily cover paneling by filling in the groves with spackling and then painting over the entire surface with primer first.

Floors

In regard to the floors, you will need to make a decision of whether to replace, repair, or clean the floors in each room. If only a few of the floors are in really bad condition, don't feel like you have to replace all the floors in the entire house.

Check floors with the level you brought to see if they are level. If the floors are not level, inspect the situation further to see if it is a flooring issue or a structural issue. It's possible that the flooring is warped, which means you just need new flooring. However, if the floor is uneven due to a structural problem, it may mean the house itself is uneven. Fixing this may involve stabilizing the structure and rebuilding parts of the foundation. While possible, rebuilding a foundation under a house is a large and expensive project. Depending on the situation, you may want to bring in a professional. Structural issues can get very expensive very quickly and may be a deal breaker when deciding whether or not to buy the house.

If the floor is wood, check for loose, cracked, or sagging floor boards. For tile floors, check for missing, loose, cracked, chipped, and broken tiles. Write down the type of tiles there are, so you can properly estimate repair costs. For carpeted rooms, inspect the overall condition of the carpet. Make a note of whether it will need to be completely replaced or just cleaned. For concrete floors, look for cracks, damage, and settled areas.

Check for joint gaps between the floor and the wall. For wood floors installed over concrete, check for soft or spongy feeling boards. This is often a sign of wood rot. Also, particularly if it is an older home, try to determine what type of floor is under carpeted areas. While you certainly cannot assume there are hardwood floors, it is important to know for estimating costs and potential profit.

Specific Rooms Throughout the House

While you'll need to inspect the floors, walls, and ceiling in every room throughout the house, there are specific rooms within the house that have additional inspection needs. The four primary rooms included in this category are the bathrooms, kitchen, attic, and basement. These rooms need special attention because they contain a large number of features that may need renovation or replacement in order to make the house sellable. Additionally, some of the most significant problems within a house can originate in these rooms.

Bathrooms

Bathrooms are very important when reselling a house. People care about the bathrooms. They care about how many bathrooms there are in a house and they care about the condition and look of the bathrooms. You will have to assume that each bathroom will need deep, intense cleaning. Aside from the cleaning, you need to pay special attention to the condition of the bathroom fixtures.

When inspecting the bathroom, determine if everything is working properly: the toilet, sink, and tub. Take a picture of the fixtures to keep in your notes. Depending on the condition and age of the fixtures, they may need replacement even if they are working properly.

Check to see if the bathroom has appropriate ventilation. If the bathroom has an exhaust fan, make sure that the fan works. If there are tiles around the tub, check for cracked, missing, loose tiles, and open joints. Check the walls around the tub or shower to see if they feel spongy or show any signs of deterioration. If there is a shower door, check to see if it opens and closes properly, has the necessary hardware, and doesn't have any cracks in the glass.

QUESTION

If there is only one bathroom, is it worth the money to add a second bathroom?
If there is only one bathroom in the house, be on the lookout for an area of the house that could be converted into a bathroom; even if it's a half-bath. Having more than one bathroom is a selling point.

Check to see if the sink and toilet are securely installed. Check to see if each fixture has its own shutoff valve. Check the plumbing under the fixtures for signs of leaks, past or present, and look for makeshift repairs. Make sure the sink and tub have proper air gaps. Check the sink drain lines for proper venting.

If there is a whirlpool, hot tub, or anything similar, check to see if it works, check the condition of the tub, check for signs of leakage, and make sure there is access to the motor, so if repairs are necessary they can be done.

Kitchen

The kitchen is arguably the most important room in the house when it comes to resale. Even people who don't cook want a kitchen that looks good and is functional. It is also, arguably, one of the most expensive rooms to renovate. Having a kitchen that looks updated is essential in the kitchen. Similar to the bathrooms, if the features of the kitchen look old and outdated, you're going to want to make changes even if they are structurally in good condition.

When inspecting the kitchen, check sinks for water flow and drainage. If there is a garbage disposal, see if it works. Check all cabinets and drawers for cracked or broken pieces and missing hardware. Make sure all the cabinets and drawers open and close easily. Check to see if all the shelves are there, level, and sturdy. Check the countertops to see if any areas are cracked, loose, warped, blistering, or burned. If there are appliances, check to see if they work and are in good condition. More than likely, appliances will need to be replaced.

ALERT

When inspecting the kitchen, check inside the cabinets, along the edges of the floor and behind or around appliances for signs of mouse or cockroach droppings. If there is a pest problem, the signs will most likely be found in the kitchen. If you are unsure of what to check for, look at pictures of pest droppings online before going into the house.

Attic

Whether the house has a full walk-up attic or just a crawlspace, it is very important to inspect it. There are several large issues such as roof leaks, fire hazards, and improper insulation that can be determined by inspecting the attic.

The first thing you want to take note of is whether or not the attic is insulated and whether it needs more insulation. Check to see if the insulation has a vapor barrier and was installed properly. Many times, people will install their own insulation to save money, but then install it incorrectly because they don't know what they are doing.

ALERT

When inspecting the attic, look for signs of nesting. Squirrels and raccoons are known to sneak into attics as a safe haven for their babies. If an animal is nesting in the attic, you will likely find a buildup of debris, which is the actual nest. You may also find droppings or food remnants in the area.

Check to see if the attic is properly ventilated and all the vents are clear. If there are boxes or furniture piled up in front of the vents, move them. Check the attic fan to see if it works. If there is an overall lack of ventilation, check for signs of damage such as the roofing boards getting warped or deteriorating. This damage can be caused by moisture buildup due to the lack of ventilation.

Check for signs of roof leaks, past or present. You will most likely be able to see if there is any water damage caused by a potential roof leak. Check around the chimney and vent stacks. These are areas where roof leaks often start. Check the rafters to see if any areas appear cracked or sagging. Look around the attic ceiling to see if there are any areas where you can see light through the ceiling.

Check to see if all the air-conditioning and heating ducts are insulated. Check the duct work for open joints. If there are plumbing stacks ending in the attic, make sure they are all capped with Air Admittance Valves (AAVs). An AAV is a one-way vent that allows you to vent the drain pipe without having a vent protrude through the roof. If these aren't present, installing an AAV is less costly and less time-consuming than installing a roof vent.

Check for any signs of makeshift wiring. This can be a real fire hazard. Makeshift wiring can usually be identified visually. You may see wires that are seemingly tangled up together. There may be wires that appear to be simply cut with a new wire attached. You may see multiple wires twisted together. Makeshift wiring is very dangerous. When electrical work is not done by someone trained to do it properly, it puts the house at risk. Makeshift or faulty wiring can cause a fire. Electric fires often start in areas like the attic or inside the walls, which means the fire can start without anyone noticing until it is too late.

Basement

The basement or crawl space, if there is one, is also an essential area to inspect thoroughly. Structural, flooding, and infestations are all issues that can be discovered when inspecting the basement.

The first thing you want to do is write down the material used for the foundation. Then inspect the foundation for cracks, missing or crumbing mortar joints, or signs of deterioration in the masonry. Look around to see if any of the walls appear to be buckling or bulging. Look to see if any portion of the basement ceiling appears to be sagging. Note long horizontal cracks in the foundation or long vertical cracks that appear to have shifted. These are all potential signs of a structural problem that you will want investigated further by a professional. Take pictures of all damage noted.

Check the basement floor for long cracks or areas where the floor appears heaved. Check for areas were the floor is damp or water is puddling, and also check the joint between the floor and the wall to see if it is cracked or if there are silt deposits. If the floor has been tiled, look for tiles that are broken, missing, loose, bulging, or deteriorating. If there is an area where all the tiles are bulging, deteriorating, or otherwise damaged, it may indicate a water problem.

FACT

Many older homes have foundations built from various types of stone that were native to the area at the time the house was built. These types of basements often have ongoing moisture problems. In these situations, keeping a dry basement is a maintenance issue, rather than something you can fix.

Check to see if the basement has sump pumps. Sump pumps are generally found in the corners of the basement on the lowest side of the property. They will be inside crocks that are installed in the floor of the basement. Sump pumps work to keep the basement from flooding if the groundwater gets to high. If it does, see if there is water in the cracks. Find out how old the sump pumps are and if they work, and also where the pumps are discharging to. Be sure to ask if the basement has been waterproofed. If it has, check to see how long ago the waterproofing was done and if there was a warranty on the work.

If there is only a crawlspace under the house, you need to check to see if the crawlspace is dry. You will get dirty. Check to make sure it is adequately ventilated and insulated, and if all the ducts and pipes in the crawl space are insulated as well.

House Utilities

The heating, ventilation, and air-conditioning (HVAC), electric, and plumbing all fall under the umbrella of utilities. These features are essential to the house and your ability to make the house sellable. Repairs to the HVAC, electric, and plumbing can also get expensive quickly. If you have concerns in any of these areas, it is best to get the advice of a professional.

HVAC

When it comes to the HVAC systems, you can inspect for obvious problems during your walkthrough, but if you have any concerns, you should consult a professional. While this may cost some money up front for a second opinion, you may save yourself grief later on by finding out something is wrong with the HVAC immediately.

The first thing you need to do is find out what type of heating system is in the house: warm-air system, hot-water system, or steam system. The second thing you need to do is find out how old the current system is. If the system is currently obsolete, you'll need to figure in the cost of a total replacement. If the system is old or highly inefficient, you'll want to consider just replacing it.

QUESTION

Is it a good investment to install central air if the house doesn't already have it?
This will depend on the area and the comparables. If the house is in a region where a good part of the year is hot, central air may be a good investment. Additionally, check the comparables in the area to see if they all have central air. You want to stay competitive with your comparables.

Go around the house and check all the supply registers. Check to make sure the dampers all open and close easily. Check the thermostat to see if it works and is in a good location. The thermostat should be in a central location of the house on an interior wall. Thermostats work by measuring the temperature of the house and then turning the heat or AC on and off as needed to maintain temperature. However, the thermostat can get false temperature readings if it is too close to typically warm areas like the kitchen or bathrooms with showers. It can also get a false reading if located on an exterior wall because it will be influenced by the outside temperature on the other side of the wall. If the thermostat is a programmable one, make sure it works properly.

For air-conditioning, you once again want to find out how old the system is. If possible, find out the last time the system was serviced. Go outside to the condenser unit and have someone turn on the air-conditioner. Listen for weird noises when the condenser unit starts up. Check to see if the fan is operating correctly. Let it run for a couple minutes to see if it appears to be running effectively. Make sure the condenser is level and on a concrete pad or blocks. See if the unit needs to be cleaned or if there are overgrown shrubs that are going to need to be cleared away from the unit. Let the air conditioning run for about fifteen minutes and then walk around the house to check the temperature and air flow coming out of each supply vent.

Electric

Just like inspecting the HVAC yourself, you can certainly do a general inspection on your own, but if your inspection leads to concerns, you should consult a professional electrician. Electrical problems can be expensive, and also dangerous if repairs are done incorrectly.

During your general inspection of the electric, start outside and check all exterior outlets to make sure they are weather protected. If the house has overhead lines, make sure they are securely attached to the house and there are no low-hanging tree branches resting on the wires. Check all exterior lights to see if they work.

Check the main panel box. If possible, find out how old it is. Check for missing plates or fuses. Check for several spare or burned out fuses. Make sure the box has at least two 20-amp appliance circuits and one 15-amp lighting circuit per 500 square feet.

Check to make sure the electrical system has adequate ground protection. Check for any types of obsolete wiring. In addition to being dangerous, these violate current electrical codes. Check the attic and basement for hanging wires, exposed spliced wires, outlets set up with extension cords, and other types of makeshift electrical repairs.

Make sure all the rooms in the house have an adequate number of outlets. There should be a minimum of one outlet for every twelve feet of wall. Make sure there are outlets in hallways. Check to see if all the outlets work. Take note of loose, broken, or missing cover plates. Take note of obvious violations such as light fixtures hanging by wires, open splices, and extension cords going through partitions or doors.

Plumbing

Plumbing goes in the same category as HVAC and electrical, insomuch that if you have any concerns, you should get a professional plumber involved. Plumbing repairs can be expensive, but plumbing problems can cause additional damage throughout the entire house.

First, you should find out if the drainage system goes through the municipal sewer, a septic tank, or a cesspool. If there is a septic tank, you need to find out when it was last cleaned out. Walk around where the septic tanks are and see if you notice any bad smells or oozing coming from the ground. These are both signs the septic system needs immediate attention. Next, find out if the property has a sprinkler system, and if it does, find out if the sprinklers work and if the supply line is protected with a vacuum breaker, which will prevent water from being siphoned backward into the water system.

Check all faucets and fixtures throughout the house to make sure they work properly. You will want to see if there are any leaks around faucets and if any of the faucets are loose. Let all the sinks, tubs, and showers run for a minute to see how well they drain. Make a note if they are draining slowly or not at all. Next, check to see if the sinks and tubs have drains that can be closed. Check the floor around the base of the toilet to see if it is spongy or has other signs of rot. Flush the toilet to make sure it fills and stops running when it is supposed to.

When you turn on each faucet to make sure it works, check the flow and pressure of both the hot and cold water. Check the pipes to see what material they are: brass, copper, galvanized iron, plastic, or a combination of these. While there are pros and cons to having each, at this point, your primary concern is cost of repairs. Brass and copper are going to be more expensive if major repairs are needed. Also check to see where the master shut off valve is and see if it works properly. Check for pipes that aren't insulated and may be vulnerable to freezing. For example, exposed pipes in basements, unheated attics, and crawlspaces are at risk of freezing. Additionally, make sure all the pipes are supported adequately.

Check the drainage pipes to see if they are sagging in any areas. Check for signs of leaking pipes, cracked pipes, or noticeably repaired pipes. Make sure the drainage pipes are pitched toward the direction they are draining, instead of being pitched back toward the source. Also make a note of what the drainage pipes are made of.

Environmental Concerns

There are a few environmental concerns you should be on the lookout for when inspecting the house. The three primary environmental concerns you need to be aware of are asbestos, lead, and mold. Asbestos and lead are problems found only in older homes since laws were put into place to protect homeowners from these concerns. Asbestos was legally banned in 1977 and lead was legally banned in 1978. Mold, however, can happen in any home, regardless of age. There are also some potential environmental concerns involving the drinking water coming into the house.

Asbestos

Asbestos is a natural fiber that has been found to be resistant to corrosion and burning; it is incredibly strong and long-lasting. For these reasons, it has been used in a wide variety of building materials including ceiling tiles, shingles, vinyl floor tiles, insulation, spackling compounds, flexible connectors, pipe insulation, and much more. The mere presence of asbestos products is not exactly a concern. However, when those products deteriorate or get damaged, asbestos fibers can be released into the air. This creates a significant environmental risk. These fibers can be breathed in by people and are known to cause cancer.

If the house you are looking at buying has asbestos-made products and you are concerned about their condition, it is best to have a professional look at them. Additionally, if asbestos products need to be removed from the house during renovations, it is best to have that done by a professional.

Lead

Lead is a significant environmental concern. Lead was a leading ingredient in house paint for years. Flaking house paint has caused lead poisoning in children all over the country. Children suffering from lead poisoning can develop learning and reading problems, while severe lead poisoning can even lead to permanent brain damage.

The levels of lead allowed in paint were drastically lowered by law in 1978, so houses built before 1978 may or may not have lead paint in them. In order to know for sure, though, the paint would need to be tested in a lab, which isn't something you can get done during an inspection. You just need to know the risk there is if you buy an older home.

If the paint is lead-based, you have several options. The lead in the paint is only inhaled or ingested if the paint is scratched, peeling, flaking, or in overall bad condition. If the paint is in perfect condition, you can simply leave it alone. If there are bad areas, you can cover those areas with gypsum board and treat that as the new wall surface. The third option is to remove the lead paint altogether. While this is the safest option, it is also the most expensive. Lead paint can only be removed by professionals trained in lead paint removal.

Mold

Although "mold" has become a hot topic word within home inspections, there are really several different types of mold, and it is only the worst type that can cause severe health problems. Most species of mold may cause a mild allergic reaction, similar to hay fever. However, all types of mold can be unsightly and have a pungent order, so regardless of the type of mold you find, you will want to remove it.

If you find mold in the house you are inspecting, make a note of the mold's location. That area will need to either be cleaned or the surface replaced. You'll also want to inspect the area more thoroughly to see how the mold grew. Mold grows as a result of moisture buildup. It is commonly found when there is poor ventilation or water leaks within the house.

Drinking Water

There are a few potential environmental concerns when it comes to the water coming into the house. The first concern is lead. If the pipes bringing water into the house are lead pipes or have lead soldering, they can be leaching lead into the water as it enters the house. If the water in the house tests positive for high levels of lead, you can have the lead pipes that are causing the problem replaced.

Another concern is sodium. If water softeners are used in the city water source or as the water comes into the home, this can dramatically increase the sodium levels in the water. While this won't affect most people, those who have other health concerns such as high blood pressure can be negatively impacted by the sodium in the water. While there isn't anything specifically you can do about this, you will need to consider it as something potential buyers may want to avoid.

ESSENTIAL

In most situations, you can't control the house's water supply. If there is a significant concern regarding the drinking water, it may be best to look for a different house to flip.

Finally, if the house's water is supplied through a well, as opposed to city water, the number of potential contaminates is nearly endless. Well water in different areas has tested positive for all types of bacteria caused by area pollution, toxic spills, and leaking septic systems.

Energy Considerations

Energy considerations are things that will make the house more energy efficient, subsequently lowering the house's monthly electric bills. Due to the rising cost of utilities, many homebuyers are looking for houses that already have energy efficient features. The amount of money you invest into energy considerations will depend on the total budget and renovation costs, but there are some basic features that should always be considered.

Doors and Windows

Doors and windows can be significant sources of energy loss. Winter heating bills and summer cooling bills will be greatly impacted by the quality of the windows and doors. With this in mind, you want to look at the age of the current windows and doors. You also want to look at their quality. If you decide the windows and doors need to be replaced, consider replacing them with more efficient options.

Insulation

Make sure the house is properly insulated. Check for areas that would benefit from more insulation and figure that into your renovation costs. Being able to tell prospective buyers that the attic was recently insulated will be a positive. In addition to wall and attic insulation, make sure all the pipes are properly insulated. This will help with energy efficiency, but it will also prevent pipes from cracking or bursting during cold months.

Possible Upgrades

Essentially, all home features have an energy-efficient version. When planning the renovations, look for ways you can make the home more energy efficient without going over budget. For example, a new thermostat is a simple upgrade that can make a big difference. Another example is the water heater. If the house already needs a new water heater, consider getting a tankless water heater. Tankless water heaters are far more efficient and will lower energy bills, which can be a selling point.

Insects and Rot

Insects and rot can cause enormous problems. They can be the difference between a profitable flip and a money pit. Both insects and rot lead to structural problems. Once the damage is done, the only resolution is to replace the damaged wood. Depending on the extent of the damage, this can be a huge endeavor. Additionally, before the repairs can be started, you have to make sure the insects are gone and the source of the rot has been addressed.

Termites

Termites live in warm and humid areas. This means they are most prevalent in the southern areas: Florida, Georgia, South Carolina, Alabama, Mississippi, Louisiana, and Southern California. However, they are also prevalent in areas that experience long periods of warmth like the Midwest and the Southwest. The areas that don't really need to worry about termites are in northern areas like Maine, Northern Minnesota, North Dakota, South Dakota, Montana, and large parts of Wyoming.

FACT

Termites actually work really slowly destroying wood, so finding evidence of termites doesn't necessarily mean there is going to be extensive damage in the house.

There are two things to look for when looking for signs of termites.

1. Look for termite tubes. Termite tubes look like lines of dirt on the outside of the foundation. These will likely be behind shrubs and close to the ground. Termite tubes can also be found along outdoor structures and fences. The termites build these to protect themselves while they're traveling and eating their way into a structure.
2. You also want to look for channels in the wood. The channels will run parallel to the grain of the wood. Along the channels you may find grayish flecks of what looks like dust. This is a combination of dirt dragged in by the bugs and termite fecal matter.

Beetles

There is a classification of beetles referred to as powderpost beetles. They are called this because their larvae feed on seasoned wood causing it to break down into a powdery residue. There are powderpost beetles that feed on hardwoods and beetles that feed on soft woods. In addition, these beetles can be found all over the world, so any wood structure is not entirely safe from these beetles.

When inspecting for powderpost beetles, you want to examine exposed wood for exit holes. These are tiny, but very clean looking holes in the wood. With an active infestation, there can easily be thirty tiny exit holes per square foot of wood surface. If the holes are dark in color, the infestation has been there for a while.

Another thing to look for during an inspection is exposed wood where the wood literally looks like it is crumbling away or deteriorating. These areas will likely also be riddled with tiny exit holes. When dealing with a beetle infestation, all damaged wood will need to be replaced.

Carpenter Ants

Carpenter ants don't actually eat the wood like other insects. They simply dig into the wood to build their colonies. These colonies damage the strength of the wood and allow moisture to get in the wood, which will lead to rot. Carpenter ant colonies, if well established, can be huge, so if one is discovered, it is important to find out the extensiveness of the colony.

When inspecting for carpenter ants, look for wood that appears to have taken in moisture or has moisture damage. You can also look for little piles of what looks like sawdust around exposed wood. As mentioned, the ants aren't eating the wood, so when they dig into it, the bits of wood simply fall.

Rot

Wood rot is caused by a fungi known as decay fungi. It works its way into the wood, weakening its structural integrity. Decay fungi can only grow on moist surfaces, so simply keeping wood clean and dry can prevent rot.

To inspect for rot, check all wood that appears moist or has been exposed to moisture. Use the screwdriver you brought to gently prod the wood. If there is rot, the wood will be fairly easy to pierce or pieces will break away. Structurally sound wood will not easily break away. Rot also makes the wood a perfect target for termites and carpenter ants, so these problems can often be found together.

CHAPTER 8

Buying a Property

Actually buying a property can be intimidating if you don't have a lot of experience doing it. You need to keep the fact that this is an investment property at the forefront of your mind, so your goal is to purchase it as inexpensively as possible in order to maximize your potential profits. Before buying a property, it is important to understand the different types of sales and how they can affect you as the buyer.

Negotiating a Price

Before jumping into a negotiation, you need to understand the market. A housing market is often described as either a seller's market or a buyer's market. A seller's market means the economy, number of houses on the market, number of people buying, bank rates, etc., are all in the seller's favor. In a seller's market, house sellers can expect higher selling prices and less restrictive terms.

ESSENTIAL

The type of market can vary from one state to another and from one city to another. You can choose to search out homes in an area that is classified as a buyer's market. As long as the drive isn't too much for you or you don't feel safe in the neighborhood, you would be better off investing in a buyer's market.

In a buyer's market, all those factors are working in the buyer's favor. This means buyers can expect to get houses at lower prices and with terms that are catering to them. Ideally, you want to buy an investment property in a buyer's market. However, if you have a set plan and stick to it, you can find a good deal in a seller's market, too.

Negotiating in a Seller's Market

Although many house flippers focus on buying bank-owned and foreclosed properties, there are plenty of privately owned properties that need to be sold as a flip due to their condition. When negotiating with a private seller, you want to be prepared walking in; have your financing already in place and make a clear offer. If your offer is below their asking price, explain the difference. For example, you can point out you are going to need to replace all the windows or replace the furnace and hot water tank. If the seller is motivated to sell, even in a seller's market, they may be more open to negotiating.

Don't ask for too much beyond being allowed to inspect and appraise the property. If you put too many contingencies into the negotiation, the seller may move on simply because they don't want to deal with you, and they have other interested buyers.

Negotiating in a Buyer's Market

A buyer's market works even more in favor of house flippers because the houses you are looking at need work. Home buyers will be more motivated to look for houses that don't need a lot of work because they can afford it in a buyer's market. When purchasing a house in a buyer's market, your initial offer should be at least 10 percent less than what you actually want to pay. A low initial offer will set the pace for the negotiation and it will let the seller know where you stand.

If the seller comes back with a counteroffer, even if it is still below what you were willing to pay, go back to them with concessions. For example, you can go back and say you'll agree to the counteroffer if they finance the closing costs. If the seller is able to cover closing costs, they may agree to this and feel good about it because you agreed to their counteroffer. Although closing costs vary depending on a wide range of factors, they can run into thousands of dollars.

Negotiating with a Bank

Negotiating with a bank is somewhat different than negotiating with a private seller. However, the market conditions will still play a role. The important thing to remember is that most banks are not interested in owning property. Therefore, when properties become bank owned, they are generally motivated to sell them. Holding on to a property does not make them any money, whatsoever. Selling the property, even at a loss, will bring in money they had otherwise lost.

Another important thing to keep in mind is that banks generally do not like accepting contract contingencies. This can even go as far as allowing an interior inspection. There are plenty of buyers willing to take the risk of buying a property without actually going inside, if the price is right. However, being new at this, your best bet is probably going to be requesting an inspection anyway.

Another important element when negotiating with a bank is to understand that they are more willing to work with buyers making cash offers. Additionally, providing proof of funding when making your offer will go a long way. This saves them the time and energy of requesting proof of funding.

Three Tips for Negotiating the Price of a House

Here are three tips for negotiating the price of a house to help you through the process.

1. **Respond quickly.** When a seller sends you a counteroffer, don't wait until the last minute to respond. Let them know quickly that you received the offer and that you will contact them once you've had the opportunity to look it over. Once you decide if you are going to accept the offer or counter again, contact the seller. Just as you don't want to wait for a response, neither will the seller.

2. **Utilize your realtor.** Before looking for a house, you worked to find a realtor you were comfortable with. You developed a relationship with this person while searching for and looking at properties. Use your realtor during your negotiations. Your realtor already understands terms and laws concerning buying and selling properties. She can clearly and effectively communicate your needs and interests during the negotiations. Plus, while you're buying and selling houses, your realtor is making money. Let her earn it by representing you to the seller.

3. **Get a list of the comparables.** Realtors are paid a percentage of the selling price. Therefore, many are more inclined to encourage higher prices. One way they do this is by using higher-end comparables that aren't exactly comparable. While, hopefully, you've found a realtor that understands your goals and the value of a long-term relationship, in the beginning, you should do your own research. Before buying a house to flip, you need to know what the house can realistically sell for, once renovated.

QUESTION

Can my realtor negotiate on my behalf when meeting with the seller?
Realtors legally cannot negotiate on anyone's behalf. They can only present offers, listen to counteroffers, and accept or decline offers when directed to by the person they represent. When offers or counteroffers are made, the realtor must present the offer to their client and wait for their response.

Common Negotiating Mistakes

Negotiating can work against you, if you aren't careful. You can end up paying too much, not getting the contingencies you want, or agreeing to terms you didn't plan on in the beginning. Here are five common negotiating mistakes people make.

1. **Not understanding the market.** If you don't know whether you are in a seller's market or a buyer's market, you may go into the negotiation with the wrong strategy, which will likely cost you the house or lead to you paying too much.
2. **Not researching the comparables.** The comparables are the other houses in the area that are similar in size and features. Looking at comparables is how you estimate the potential selling price for the house, once it is renovated. If you pay too much for the house, you won't be able to make money off the flip.
3. **Telling the seller too much.** Being able to buy a house with cash is great for you, but you don't want to tell a private seller up front that you plan to pay cash. That sends the message that you have plenty of money, and the seller may be less likely to negotiate the price with you. Now, this is actually the opposite when negotiating with a bank. If you are able to pay cash, you want to let them know upfront along with proof of funding.
4. **Not making your options clear.** You can't go into a negotiation determined to get a particular house. You want to let the seller know that you've been looking at a lot of houses and that there are a lot of good prospects. This tells the seller that you are going to buy a house, whether it is their house or not. They will be more motivated to win you over if they know you are looking at other houses.
5. **Getting too emotional.** This is particularly true when buying through an auction. You need to decide how much you are willing to pay based on your available financing and the potential profit for the home. If the price of the house goes over the amount you decided to pay, you need to be willing to walk away. Getting caught up in the excitement of bidding will lead to you paying too much and not making a profit on the flip.

Discussing Terms

The terms of a sale can include a wide variety of things such as the closing date, closing costs, appraisals, inspections, selling price, and contingencies. Terms are all the elements you can negotiate when buying a property. Terms other than the actual price have value and can be an important part of the negotiation.

Closing Costs and Date

There are always costs associated with selling a house. These include the costs associated with the needed paperwork and processing. The amount of the closing costs may vary dramatically; however, it is important to keep in mind they can easily be thousands of dollars. Who pays the closing costs is an important term to negotiate. For example, as a buyer, you can agree to a slightly higher price in return for the seller paying the closing costs.

The closing date can also be negotiated. As a house flipper, your clock starts as soon as you take possession of the property. If you know you can't get started until a certain date, you should take that into consideration when negotiating. For example, you can propose that the house doesn't close until the following month as part of your negotiations.

Contingencies

Contingencies are "if" statements. For example, you agree to the selling price *if* the seller agrees to pay $2,500 toward a new roof. This can also apply to the appraisal and inspection. For example, you can agree to the selling price "pending an inspection." This means you reserve the right to renegotiate the price after the house is inspected in case you find something seriously wrong that will affect your potential profits. Generally speaking, if you are negotiating with a bank, you aren't going to be able to negotiate contingencies. However, if you are negotiating with a private seller, you can request as many contingencies as you want, as part of the negotiations.

Types of Sales

There are several different types of sales, other than private sales, that are often ideal for flips. There are houses that have been abandoned or are about to be abandoned. They might be owned by a bank or lender, or they are in the process of foreclosure. Oftentimes, negotiations are influenced by the type of sale. It is important to understand the difference between these types of sales in order to have a negotiation strategy going into the potential deal.

Pre-Foreclosure Sales

A pre-foreclosure sale is when the homeowners are still in possession of the house, but they are delinquent on their payments and the house will go into foreclosure if it isn't sold or the owners can't come up with the money. Pre-foreclosure sales can be lengthy and grueling, in terms of negotiation. In many cases, the homeowners are resistant because they feel they are being forced into selling and moving, or they still want to make a profit on the sale of their house.

However, this is not always the case. The sellers may be very motivated to sell because they've accepted the move and don't want a foreclosure on their credit report. Really, they could go either way. Additionally, you may be able to find a pre-foreclosure house in your price range that needs fairly little renovation because it was cared for very well. Work with your realtor to see what your options are in the area you want to buy a house.

The important thing to keep in mind is that the sellers will need to get at least what they still owe on the house. If they have not yet pursued the option of a short sale, their bottom line might be more than you want to spend. In these situations, negotiations aren't really effective because the seller's hands are tied. However, if you are really interested in the house, you may propose the idea of seeing if their bank will agree to a short sale.

Short Sales

A short sale is when a property is selling for less than what is actually owed on the house. This may include the balance on the mortgage, as well as any liens that have been put in place against the property. When a home-owner is unable to repay the full amount that they owe through the sale of the property, the lien holders may agree to settle for a lesser amount. The unpaid balance is then considered a deficiency against the homeowner.

Short sales are typically allowed when the alternative is a foreclosure. Although not the full amount, a short sale allows the lender to recover at least a portion of the money they are owed. From the prospective of a house flipper, short sales can be tricky to negotiate. You would be working with both the homeowner and the lender to agree on terms. Because of the unique situation, you can still try to negotiate other terms in addition to the price.

ESSENTIAL

Short sales work differently than other types of sales. It is important that you are working with a realtor that has experience doing short sales. This will make the transaction process faster and with less problems.

The bank will want to get as much as it can out of the deal. The homeowners may be resistant to agree to a short sale if they think they can sell the house for a price over the loan amount. Being able to sell the house for a comparable asking price would allow them to walk away with some money. Additionally, short sales leave a negative mark on the homeowner's credit report, which may make him or her resistant to the deal. Buying through a short sale can also be a lengthy process.

Despite these risks, short sales can allow you to get a house in good condition and in a good neighborhood for a good price. This would allow you to make a fast turnaround and subsequently, a fast profit, on the investment. Every situation and property is different, so it is important to go into every situation with an open mind. Just as the bank will have their bottom line, you need to have your price limits in mind before talking to them about a short sale price.

Sheriff Sales and Auctions

A sheriff sale or auction happens after a house has been foreclosed on. The bank puts the house up for auction as a means to sell it and get back the money they are owed. There are pros and cons to house auctions. The biggest pro is that it is relatively easy to get a house at a really good price at an auction. Houses can be auctioned off for significantly less than they are worth because the lenders don't want to remain in possession of the house. They just want to get back some of the money they were owed on the property.

The biggest downside to buying a house at an auction is that you are not typically allowed to see the interior of the house prior to the auction. You agree to buy the house "as-is." This means you are unable to inspect the interior of the house prior to buying it, and if you discover major problems after buying it, you don't have any recourse against the bank that sold you the house.

FACT

In many areas, house auctions are conducted online and in person, simultaneously. That means you can participate in the auction even if you aren't able to be there. You can also choose to send a representative to bid on your behalf.

Buying a house at an auction is a greater risk than simply flipping a house. For some, this makes it even more appealing. If you are a risk-taker, then this is certainly something to consider. If you are looking for a safer route, you'll want to avoid buying uninspected houses.

Although you aren't able to enter the house during an auction, you can do some research on the house to learn as much as you can. For example, you can check the County Auditor's website to see who the previous owner was and then contact the owner to see if they would be willing to talk to you about the house. While this is a bold move, if you are really interested in the house, it is feasible.

You can also conduct an exterior inspection of the house. You will be allowed to look into the windows of the house, too, if they aren't covered. You can talk to the neighbors to see how long the house has been empty and if they know of any major work done on the house before it was foreclosed. You can learn a lot about a house without actually entering it.

You don't get to negotiate during an auction, you just bid on the house against other potential buyers. Auctions can be as unique as the houses for sale. Some auctions will not have any bids on the property, while other auctions will have a few potential buyers eagerly bidding against each other.

The key thing to remember when going to an auction is that you can't go over your price limit. Sometimes the energy and spirit of an auction can make people act competitively. You might feel inclined to go over your budget because you really want to "win" the auction. However, you need to keep your end goal in mind and protect your potential profits by not paying too much for the property.

Real Estate Owned (REO) Properties

A property is consider REO when it has been foreclosed on and didn't sell at auction. At this point, the bank owns the property. REO properties cost banks money because they have to provide minimal maintainance for the property to stay within city regulations and they are not receiving any income for the property.

ALERT

REO homes are arguably the most attractive for potential investors. If you see an REO home that you are interested in buying, you need to prepare a proposal quickly and get it submitted. If the house is really good, there are likely going to be other investors who are interested.

REO properties often represent great investment opportunities because banks are motivated sellers. Since the banks do not want to own properties, investors can get good prices for the houses they are interested in. The downside of buying REO properties is that banks are generally not willing to negotiate a lot of terms, and they are generally more motivated to work with investors paying cash for the properties.

When submitting a proposal for an REO property, it is important to submit your proposal in writing and include proof of funding. The more prepared you are with your proposal and the more prepared you are to take possession of the house, the more willing the bank will be to work with you. In your proposal, it is important to clearly state the price you are offering for the property with an explanation of the price. For example, you can provide an estimate of how much it will cost to renovate the house and a summary of some of the major renovations that will be needed.

CHAPTER 9

Types of Renovations to Consider

When considering what needs to be done to the house you purchase, it is important to remember it is not the house you are going to live in. It is the house you want to make as much money with as you can. With that in mind, you need to make a list of the renovations you are going to do. Create a plan for the entire house before you get started. Although some things may change along the way, you need to have somewhere to start.

Deciding What Needs to Be Renovated

From your inspection notes, make a list of all the renovations you think the house will need. To keep it organized, you can create the list going room by room. Add every possible renovation. Even if you don't think you'll have the budget for something, add it to the list. It can always be eliminated later.

Your renovation list can be simple and handwritten to start. At this point you are still very much brainstorming; nothing you think of is set in stone. Here is an example of how a proposed renovation list might look.

LIVING ROOM

- New carpeting
- Repaint walls
- Light switch plate needs to be replaced
- Open up wall between living room and dining room
- Trim around bay window needs to be replaced
- Piece of trim behind door is missing and needs to be replaced
- All trim needs repainting

FRONT HALL

- Remove crown molding (it doesn't match anything else in the house)
- Repaint walls
- Repair wall at base of steps
- Replace light fixture

As you can see from the sample, the list of repairs aren't in complete sentences or explained further. It is just a list of the renovations you think of based on your observations of the house and what would make it look better. You can make the list more detailed than the sample; it is up to you. The point is that creating the list does not need to be a complicated process. Additionally, the list can be refined, expanded, or edited as you move forward.

There is an old saying, "Don't put lipstick on a pig." This sentiment can easily be applied to houses being flipped. Don't try to hide the major problems with cosmetic changes. Always fix the problems first, then make it look nice.

Exterior Renovations

Exterior renovations can often be done simultaneously with interior renovations. Scheduling things to happen simultaneously will enable you to get the total renovations done faster, so you should schedule things whenever you can. Exterior renovations will include renovations to the exterior of the house as well as the property. Focus on the major renovations first. Here is a sample list of possible exterior renovations you'll be considering.

- New roof
- New exterior wall covering/repairs to exterior walls
- New windows
- Repairs to the walkways, driveway, etc.
- Repairs to the property and landscape
- Repairs to outdoor structures
- Demolition of outdoor structures
- Repairs to porch, patio, or deck
- Exterior painting
- Reseeding the back yard
- Pulling out the bushes along the side of the house

Once you have a complete list of all the possible renovations to do to the exterior of the house, you need to prioritize the list. This way, if you go over budget and need to make cuts, you are already know which are the least important renovations that you can cut. For example, a new roof when the current roof is leaking is more important than leveling a deck that is slightly dipped in the corner. You don't want to fix the deck first because the dip bothers you and then not have enough money to fix the roof. Additionally, having the prepared list will help you decide which renovations need a total replacement and which renovations simply need a repair.

Interior Renovations

Interior renovations can be written up room by room, and should include both repairs and cosmetic renovations. You can add your "wish list" renovations to this list as well. The wish list renovations are the things you would like to do if you have the money and time to complete them, but truly are optional if you run out of either.

For example, you may think built-in cabinets would look great in the master bath and add to the overall storage. Or you may think adding a skylight to the dining room will really brighten up the place and make it feel more welcoming. While these types of renovations are unneeded, they may add to the perceived value of the house and help it to sell faster. However, you should not sacrifice something that needs to be done just so they can be completed.

Utilities

Making sure all the utilities are in safe and solid working order is essential. This will involve getting professionals in the house to look everything over and make any needed repairs. Utility renovations can get expensive quickly, so it is important to get estimates for any problems identified during the inspection ahead of time. Because these types of repairs need to be done by a professional, they will need to be scheduled. It is best to get them scheduled as soon as possible in case the contractor has another job to finish first.

Making Needed Repairs

All necessary utility repairs will have to be done. The utilities need to be up to code as well as functional. It will be basically impossible to sell a house without working plumbing or lights. Get an estimate for all the needed repairs. However, before making the needed repairs, you may want to look into any upgrades you can get while getting the repair work done. It is important to think about upgrades early for this reason: if a plumber is going to open up the walls to make needed repairs, you don't want them to put everything back together and then have to open it up again because you decided to upgrade something.

ALERT

In addition to being the right thing to do, when it comes to utility repairs or upgrades, you may have to go through a city inspection to ensure everything is up to code.

The needed repairs are the priority, but take the time to discuss possible upgrades with your contractors. There are plenty of upgrades that will add to the perceived value of the house without being drastically more expensive.

Making Upgrades

Upgrading the utilities can do a lot to increase the perceived value of the house. Obviously, in most situations, upgrades will mean spending more money. It is important to weigh the additional costs with the perceived value to potential buyers. For example, if you need to replace a water heater anyway, it is worth looking at tankless water heater options. Depending on the size of the house, these can actually be very cost effective. Additionally, they will significantly reduce the monthly utilities, which is very desirable for potential buyers. Take a look at the comparables. If your house is pretty much on par with the other available houses, something like a tankless water heater can be the thing that puts your house over the top for potential buyers.

Other examples of upgrades regarding the utilities include installing LED lighting. LED lighting costs less on a monthly basis and provides better light than traditional lighting. You can add additional light fixtures throughout the house. If the master bath only has a single vanity, you can add a second sink and create a double vanity. If the house comes with window air conditioners, you can upgrade to central air. There are numerous ways you can upgrade the utilities in a house. While brainstorming possible upgrades, it is important to talk to your contractors, but it will also be helpful to look at your comparables again. Take an afternoon to tour a few of the comparables in your area. What kinds of amenities do they have that you, too, could easily upgrade during the renovation process? This is the type of question you need to have in mind while looking at other houses for sale.

Cosmetic Repairs

Cosmetic repairs refers to the renovations that need to be done to make the house sellable, but aren't actually fixing anything. For example, the entire interior of the house may need to be painted. This may not mean there is any actual damage to the walls. However, if the walls are really ugly or dirty looking, the house is not going to sell. Putting a fresh coat of paint on everything will make the house brighter, better looking, and more appealing to potential buyers. Cosmetic repairs may include the following things.

- Painting
- Refinishing ceilings
- New flooring
- New or updated cabinets in the kitchen and bathrooms
- Removal of wallpaper, paneling, or other wall coverings
- Installing new light fixtures

Essential Repairs

Although cosmetic, some repairs are essential to selling the house. One of these repairs, which was already mentioned, is painting. It will be rare that you'll flip a house and not need to repaint the entire interior. Even if the paint wasn't too bad when you bought it, after weeks of renovations, the walls are bound to be bumped into, scuffed up, and dirty. Fresh flooring is also essential. Similarly to the condition of the walls, it will be rare that you will flip a house where the carpeting is salvageable. In most situations, all carpeting will need to be replaced. Hard floors will either need to be replaced, refinished, or thoroughly scrubbed.

What Really Makes the Difference

When it comes to cosmetic renovations, the two most important rooms are the kitchen and the bathrooms. If you are going to spend extra money in any room, you will get the greatest benefit from spending more money on these rooms. For the bathrooms, new vanities and fixtures will go a long way. In the kitchen, the newer and fresher it looks, the better. If your budget allows, consider replacing or refinishing the cabinets, installing a new counter top, or making the needed changes to increase the size of the kitchen.

Replacing the front door with a 20-gauge steel door can make a real difference. According to reports by MSN, this particular change offers a 73 percent return on investment.

Landscaping

The biggest thing you need to worry about with your landscaping decision, is that it appears easy to maintain. You want to make sure the yard is as level as possible without any holes. You want all the trees and bushes on the property trimmed down so they look easy to maintain. If the grass is not lush and green looking, you should consider reseeding the lawn or using Weed N' Feed to revive the grass already there.

Be sure to work on the lawn after all the exterior renovations are complete, and you're sure you won't have any equipment or delivery trucks driving over the grass. This will prevent you from having to do work over and it will leave the lawn looking its best.

What Areas to Focus On

The better the property looks, the more enticing it will be to potential buyers. The front yard and entrance area will be the first thing potential buyers see, so you want to make sure the walkway is repaired and even. If there is no place along the walkway to plant flowers, put some flower pots with fresh flowers near the entranceway to brighten it up as people approach the house. The grass should be nicely mowed for each showing and open house, and if flowers start looking dead, pull them out and plant some new ones.

When Less Is More

When it comes to decorative landscape, you don't want to go overboard. The more flowers, shrubs, plants, and bushes you have in the landscape, the more maintenance will be needed to maintain the yard. This can deter a lot of home buyers. Keeping the landscape decorative but simple will appeal to a larger number of people. Additionally, a lot of landscaping will crowd the front of the house. You want to make sure the focus of the curb appeal is the house and the front entrance.

ALERT

If there is a critter problem in the yard causing holes or uneven landscape, it is best to get rid of the critter problem before repairing the landscape. New holes can appear overnight if they the critter is still there.

Outbuildings

The renovations you make to outbuildings (shed, detached garage, etc.) will depend on a lot of factors. The first thing you will need to decide is if the outbuildings are worth renovating. Many times, exterior garages, sheds, and barns are rundown and left in seriously ill repair. If the outdoor structure basically needs to be rebuilt, but adds little monetary value to the property, it is best to just eliminate it. Tear the structure down and plant grass. It will eliminate a problem and make the yard look bigger.

Consider the Selling Points

When making renovation decisions regarding outbuildings, focus on the selling points. For example, running electricity to a detached garage that is in otherwise great condition will enhance the perceived value of the property. More than likely, a prospective homeowner won't think twice about there being electricity. However, if they are told there isn't any electricity to the garage, it will suddenly become a flaw of the property.

Another possible renovation or addition would be adding a floor to a shed or detached garage that has a dirt floor. Adding a floor will increase the appeal of the outbuilding. You want to look at the outbuildings with the buyer in mind. Ask yourself what the buyer would be discouraged by when they see it, and then fix it. Painting is a simple way of sprucing up an outbuilding. Depending on what the outbuilding is and how close it is to the house, you can also add some plants or shrubs that coordinate with the rest of the landscaping to the front of the outbuilding to create a visual connection between the house and outbuilding.

Adding Outbuildings

Another thing to consider is if you should add an outbuilding to the property. For example, if you have a property without a garage, you may want to add a shed for outside storage. You don't want a potential buyer to look at the property and wonder where they are going to store the lawnmower and grill. Outside storage is essential, so if the house doesn't have any, you need to budget for creating some. You don't need to spend a lot of money adding outside storage. Even a small shed is better than no shed at all.

QUESTION

What if the yard really isn't big enough for a shed?
You can also add an outdoor closet to the back of the house. It can be attached to the house, and just big enough to fit a lawnmower.

Appliances

One thing you can choose to do is install appliances in the kitchen before putting the house on the market. Whether or not you choose to include appliances may depend entirely on your available budget. The refrigerator and stove are completely optional. However, there are a few appliances you should seriously consider. If there is space in the kitchen for a dishwasher, having one already installed will increase the perceived value of the house. A garbage disposal is another small appliance that people often look for in a home.

The Advantages and Disadvantages of Including Appliances

If the potential buyers already have appliances that they like, they won't be interested in the house coming with appliances. However, if they don't have appliances or if they want newer appliances, this might be a huge appeal. One way you can mitigate this concern would be to include appliances during staging, but leave it up to the buyers if they are interested in keeping the appliances. They can be used as a contingency during negotiations if they are interested. If the buyer is not interested in the appliances, you can hold onto them for your next flip.

How to Save Money on Appliances

If you do choose to include appliances, there are a few things you can do to cut costs. First, you can look into buying appliances straight from a supplier. You can also buy appliances that are on sale or clearance. Many big box stores, like Best Buy and Lowe's, will clearance out appliances that have been returned, even if there is nothing wrong with them.

CHAPTER 10

The Renovation Process

The renovation process can go in several different directions. It will depend primarily on how involved you are with the actual renovations. This will include creating timelines that coordinate the schedules of all your contractors. If you are planning to be personally involved in the renovation process as opposed to working with a general contractor, you need to schedule when you will be at the property. In order to stay on top of the project and ensure everything is done in a timely manner and up to your standards, you should plan to be there on a daily basis. While flipping houses can be done in addition to having a regular job, you need to have the time to commit to the project or the money to hire a general contractor.

Major Renovations versus Cosmetic Renovations

You are going to be dealing with two basic types of renovations: major and cosmetic. While these have already been introduced, it is important to understand the difference. Additionally, there are going to be renovations that can be categorized as major and cosmetic. For example, if the house needs new siding, this is both a major and cosmetic change. Siding that is damaged or in overall poor condition can cause water damage to the wall beneath. However, siding that is damaged, faded, and unsightly can also negatively effect the perceived value of the house.

Major Renovations

Major renovations include the changes you make that go beyond the way the house looks. This would include major repairs to any part of the house like a new roof, new siding, electrical work, or changing the floor plan. Major renovations, generally speaking, need to be done first. Keep in mind that these major renovations aren't necessarily the most expensive renovations on your list. Cosmetic renovations can also be costly.

Major renovations will be more likely to include work with contractors. The major renovations are hierarchically more important, so they have to take preference in the budget. When allocating how much money will be spent on various projects, it is essential that the major renovations that need to be done are included in the budget.

Oftentimes what is really going to sell a house is the wow factor you create when prospective buyers walk through. Look for ways to create that wow factor in your flip. This can be as simple as a new front door, better lighting, or high-end counter tops. The key to the wow factor is to include something that isn't typically found in comparably priced houses.

Cosmetic Renovations

Cosmetic renovations are improvements that will make the house look nicer and sell faster. This type of renovation includes cleaning out the house, painting, replacing light fixtures, replacing plate covers, and trim. Cosmetic changes can also include new cabinets in the kitchen or bathrooms, new flooring, or new window treatments.

Cosmetic renovations often feel like busy work—like going through the house and replacing plate covers. However, the cosmetic changes are vital to the success of the project because they are the things the prospective buyers are going to be seeing. While you can tell a prospective buyer the entire house was recently rewired, they are going to be looking at the new kitchen floor and the freshly painted living room.

Renovating with a Buyer in Mind

It is important to keep the buyer in mind when renovating the house. This isn't going to be your house, so you don't want to stick with the renovations you would like done if you were living there. You need to keep the colors and designs neutral and calm. When spending money on major renovations, you need to consider the prospective of the buyer. For example, if the floor plan has several closed off rooms, you might be better off taking out a couple walls and creating an open floor plan. Open floor plans are very popular and a lot of buyer's look for them.

Keeping the End Result in Mind

An important part of renovating a house is being able to visualize the final product. While a lot of people can't look at a dirty, rundown, old house and see the potential—you need to be able to. You also need to be able to make your vision a reality in order to sell the renovated house. If you have trouble mentally visualizing the potential, have a more experienced house flipper walk through the property with you and point out things they would do if flipping the house.

Evaluating the Importance of a Renovation

Every renovation you do is a decision. You decide if the roof needs new shingles or if they can just be cleaned. You decide if the house needs another half bath or if the two already in the house are enough. For each renovation, you need to decide if it is valuable to the house.

- Will it increase the perceived value of the house to potential home buyers?
- Will it make your house stand out among the comparables?
- Will the money being spent on the renovation pay off in the end?

Where to Start

Once you officially buy the house and you are handed the keys, you might feel a little overwhelmed. There are a million things to do and they are all running through your head. The first thing you need to do is create your game plan. Your game plan includes your budget and your timeline. If you haven't started already, you need to start scheduling your contractors to arrive when their portion of the house will be ready to be worked on.

ALERT

You've probably heard the phrase "Don't put the cart before the horse." That phrase perfectly applies to the house flipping process. Although you might be really eager to get started the minute you have the keys in your hand, moving forward without a game plan can cost you both time and money.

If there is garbage, furniture, or other stuff in the house, the first thing you need to do is clean out the house. This includes ripping out anything that has to go before renovations can start, like carpeting, fixtures, walls, etc. This is the demolition portion of the work, and it needs to be done first. During this phase of the work, it is essential to always wear gloves and safety goggles for your personal safety.

Making a Priority List

Go over your list of renovations and put them in order by priority. Top priority jobs should be the ones that are going to take awhile and will hold up other jobs, so you need to start them early. For example, if you are having a couple walls built to alter the floor plan, that needs to be done before you can do any painting, flooring, molding, installing fixtures, etc.

Getting the top priority jobs started right away will ensure they are done quickly and there is time for improvements, if needed. Beyond the top priority ones will be the jobs that are big. For example, if you are replacing all the cabinets in the kitchen, it is a big job, so you want to get that started as soon as you can.

The smaller and cosmetic renovations come after the major renovations. Even if you feel compelled to start cosmetic renovations, hold off until the house is ready. Cosmetic changes make the house look finished, so you don't want to risk damaging cosmetic changes because you weren't done with the major renovations. For example, if you paint a room and then it is discovered that a wall needs to be opened up for electrical or plumbing work, you just wasted the time, energy, and money spent painting the room.

Creating a Schedule

Creating a schedule for a house renovation can be a lot of work, but the more you understand about the needed renovations, the easier it will get. Creating a schedule will allow you to know exactly when your contractors will be there to work. This will allow you to ensure there aren't too many contractors in the house at once or that the renovations are being done in the wrong order.

Working with Contractors

There are two important things you need to discuss with your contractors when creating your work schedule for the project: how much it will cost and how long it will take for them to complete the project. It is also important to talk to your contractors about their availability. Then, you must commit to a timeframe.

Many contractors are working multiple jobs simultaneously. Many are even running multiple crews simultaneously. You need to explain to the contractor your expectations that they will be there when they say they will be there and once they start your project, they will finish it. One of the most frustrating things that can happen when working with a contractor is when they show up to start your project and then don't come back for several days because they are trying to finish up someone else's project.

What do you do if a contractor is not sticking to the schedule?
There are a couple of ways to approach this problem. First, you talk to the contractor to figure out what the problem is. If the problem is within his control, you can request a discount for the time lost due to his inability to stick to the schedule. Depending on how that goes, you can also choose to cut your losses and contact another contractor.

Working Them Into Your Schedule

Once you know when your contractor can start and how many days it will take his crew to complete the job, you can work them into the schedule you are creating. Start with the contractors of the major renovations and work your way down to the contractors you are using for the cosmetic renovations.

Make sure the schedule is reasonable and the house is prepared for the contractors when they arrive. If for any reason a contractor needs to be pushed back, call that contractor immediately to work out a new schedule. Developing relationships with contractors is important and if you waste their time, they will not value you as a customer.

Negotiating Costs

Don't be afraid to negotiate with contractors. Start by asking for a breakdown of their estimate so you know how much of the price they gave you is materials and how much is labor. This will give you a jumping off point for negotiations. Additionally, if you aren't happy with the price they offered, don't be afraid to get an estimate from another contractor. Let them each know you are shopping around for the best price.

What to Do Yourself

A lot of people that get into house flipping have some previous experience in renovations or home improvement, and they are interested in being an active part of the renovation process. You may want to do the renovations yourself, or at least most of the renovations. Doing renovations yourself can obviously save you a lot of money that would otherwise be spent on paying contractors. If you have the time and the know-how, you should certainly do as much work as you can on the flip.

Knowing When to Hire Someone

There are times when you need to hire contractors. Hiring contractors is important when you don't have the expertise needed to do the project correctly or when doing it yourself will cost you more in time than hiring a contractor.

When the renovations include specialized jobs like electrical work, plumbing, or HVAC, you need to bring in a professional to ensure they are done correctly and safely. For small jobs, like replacing a fuse or installing a ceiling fan, you may be able to handle them yourself. For larger jobs, like replacing a fuse box or rewiring a room, you will probably need a professional.

FACT

Generally speaking, people are resistant to outsourcing work they know they can do themselves. However, the fact of the matter is, you will be more productive focusing on the tasks that are your strengths rather than spending time on everything else.

You also need to consider hiring a professional when the time it will take you to complete a job will be significantly longer than if you just have a professional come in and do it. For example, you may know how to install vinyl siding; however, it would take you two weeks to do it because you aren't a professional and you just have one other person helping you. If you hire a professional, they could get the job done in three days. It is worth the money to hire a professional if the two weeks it will take you is holding up the rest of the renovations or the sale of the house.

Balance Time and Money

An important part of knowing when to hire someone and when to do it yourself is understanding the time-money balance. You want to save money doing the renovations, but you also need to get the house back on the market as quickly as possible. In most cases, it will be a judgment call. You need to decide how much money your time is worth. If it would take you twenty hours to complete a task that you could have hired out for $200, you need to decide if your time is worth more than ten dollars per hour, because that is how you'd be valuing your time.

The Importance of Documentation

Documenting everything you do with the house is important for multiple reasons. First, you need to track all of your expenses and income for taxes. What you make selling the house will be counted as part of your income for tax purposes. For that reason, you need to keep documentation of every dollar you spend in order to include it as a deduction. Additionally, if after filing your taxes you get audited, you need proof of all the money you claim to have spent.

Documentation is also important when trying to sell the house. Prospective buyers may want proof of features you claim to have recently replaced. If there were warranties on any of the work done in the house, the new owners will also need copies of the warranty information.

Finally, keeping all your documentation organized will enable you to stay on top of the renovation process. You'll have quick access to all the contact information for your contractors and the contracts you signed with them. You will also know how much is being spent as you spend it. Tracking expenses during the renovation process will let you know immediately if you are going over budget in any particular areas. This knowledge will allow you to respond appropriately to get the project back on budget.

What You Need to Keep

There are a variety of things you need to keep as part of the documentation process. It is best to get a binder for each house. This will allow you to keep things separate when you are working on multiple flips, but it will also help you to keep everything in place during the project and portable. You can keep the binder with you in your vehicle as you are traveling back and forth to the house.

Losing receipts, contracts, contacts, etc., can cost you a significant amount of money. It can deter potential buyers, and it can get you in trouble with the IRS. Create an effective filing system before you even get started because the paper is going to start piling up quickly.

Here is a list of things you will need to keep during the flip.

1. Your copies of all the paperwork associated with the purchase of the property.
2. The contact information for all your contractors, inspector, vendors, supplies, etc.
3. Any contracts you signed with realtors, contractors, or vendors.
4. Receipts for everything you spend. This includes tools, supplies, materials, rental equipment, business meals, utilities, contractors, etc. All money spent as a result of the flip needs to be accounted for.
5. Warranty information on any work being done.
6. Product information on things like new roofs, new furnaces, new central air, etc. These are things that will eventually be passed on to the new owners.
7. Before pictures you took after buying the property but before the renovations started.

How to Keep It Organized

As mentioned, it is best to get a three-ring binder at the start of the project. You can then three-hole punch items to stick them in the binder, or add clear page protectors to hold on to receipts and smaller papers. Divide the binder into sections based on the work you are getting done. For example, you can have a section for rental equipment, supplies, materials, etc. You can also have a section for each contractor you are working with, so everything associated with that part of the job goes in that section.

You should also get a large mailing envelope, three-hole punch it, and stick it in the very front of the binder. Throughout your day, if you stop and buy something for the project or you meet someone and get a business card, you can stick everything in the large envelope. Then at the end of each day, when you are relaxed, you can go through the envelope, record the receipts with your expenses, and put everything in the appropriate section of the project binder. This will help you to stay on top of recording expenses, and it will make sure you aren't losing receipts by sticking them in your wallet, pocket, or leaving them in a bag somewhere.

Ways to Save Money Without Cutting Corners

One of the easiest ways to reduce expenses is to closely monitor and control the cost of renovations. There are numerous ways you can work to save money on renovations without doing so at the expense of the finished house. You don't want the house to look like you were cutting corners or only using the cheapest materials. You need to cut corners creatively. This includes working to get the best deals on supplies and materials, reusing materials that are still good, and working with your suppliers to get discounts on the things you need.

Buying What Is Most Cost-Effective

You don't have to buy the cheapest option. In fact, in many cases, you don't want to buy the cheapest option because it will look like the cheapest option. However, you also don't have to buy the same quality or style you would buy for your own home. You can shop for what is on sale, clearance, or discounted for another reason.

For example, you'll be painting the interior of the house in neutral colors. Most stores like Lowe's and Home Depot have what they call, "mis-tints." These are gallons of paint that a customer ordered, but the color didn't come out exactly how they wanted it. Before paying full price for paint, ask to see what mis-tints they have available. If there are multiple gallons of a neutral color, start with those and then buy more paint to match. You can usually get a gallon of mis-tint paint for five dollars, which is a fifteen to twenty dollar discount (or more) per gallon.

Another thing to look for is returned, special order carpet. Once a store measures and cuts a piece of carpet, they can't resell it at regular price, so if a customer refuses it for any reason, the store has to sell the piece of carpeting at a discount. Before paying full price for carpet, go to the store with all of your needed room measurements, and ask to see the returned or discounted carpeting.

ESSENTIAL

Reusing materials already found in the house can save you money, but it can also be a selling point for a lot of buyers. Generally speaking, people like creative repurposing. They like to hear about it and they like to tell other people about it when it is in their own home.

Reusing Materials

When cleaning out and demolishing parts of the house, don't just send everything straight to the dumpster. Watch for things that can be reused. For example, if you are moving walls to change the layout of rooms, pull out the good baseboards and molding and set them aside. That way, if you need to replace molding or baseboards in another room, you already have some that match the current boards. You'll be repainting everything anyway, so you won't need to worry about them being different colors or in different conditions.

Examine tubs, sinks, and toilets to decide if they really need replacing or if they can just be cleaned or refinished. Examine kitchen cabinets to see if they are in good structural shape. Cabinets can be refinished, repainted, or you can even have the doors replaced. Fixing and refinishing what is already there, in most cases, is less expensive than replacing them. Even if you decide to replace the kitchen cabinets because they look really bad, keep the cabinets that are still usable and install them somewhere else like the basement. This will increase available storage and the perceived value.

Lighting is another area where you can save money. If you are removing lighting fixtures from a room, hold on to them until you are done with the project in case you need lighting fixtures in another area and the ones you removed will work. Also keep in mind that if a lighting fixture still works, but is unsightly, you can replace the globe, glass, fan blades, etc., to make it look better, more current, and new.

Working with Resale Stores

Check your area for resale stores that specialize in building materials. For example, the Habitat for Humanity has a chain of stores that they call "Restores." These are resale stores that specialize in selling building materials, tools, fixtures, and more. Everything is donated, and the money from selling things goes to support Habitat for Humanity's mission to provide houses for people in need. In a Restore, you will find things that are new, still in the box, things that are new but open, and items that are used but still usable. If you have one in your area, go with your shopping list, you will likely find a lot of the items you are going to need in your renovation.

You should also check in your area to see if there are any commercial renovation companies. Many companies that renovate places like hotels, office buildings, and large apartment complexes remove and resell the materials and fixtures that are still usable. This allows them to recoup money on their expenses. Sometimes these companies will have warehouse style stores that you can look around in. Other times, they have planned sales, where the public is invited to come buy stuff on a specific day. If you do have a company like this in your area, they would be a good contact to network with and try to build a professional relationship.

Buying in Bulk

Oftentimes, when working with a supply store or vendor, you can get a discount for buying items in bulk. If a discount is not automatically offered on bulk purchases, feel free to ask for one. These types of businesses value professional relationships and networking; discounts can often be provided as a way to encourage loyalty.

ALERT

Don't just assume because you are buying something in bulk that it is more cost effective than buying in smaller quantities. Check the per unit price when buying more than one item.

This can also be true when items are on clearance. For example, if a particular toilet is on clearance and they only have three left, you can ask for an additional discount if you agree to buy all three. While you may only need two for the house you are currently working on, if the price is good enough, you might be able to get three for less than the regular price of two.

Utilizing Your Relationships

By the time you've started renovations, you have hopefully developed some professional relationships with contractors, vendors, and suppliers. You can utilize those relationships to save you money on a project. Contact the people you've worked with and discuss the supplies you are going to need for the house. See if they can get you a discount if you buy it all from them, or if they know of materials on clearance that are on your list.

As you do more flips, you can keep a standing list with your contact for supplies you need on a regular basis. These are items the store can watch out for and contact you if the items go on sale or clearance. While it might seem like a lot to ask, professionals in these types of businesses are often eager to help because it allows them to grow their business and their network of professional contacts.

CHAPTER 11

Green Options in Renovations

Being "green" is a hot issue in the current housing market. While marketing a house as green may not be possible due to the legal definition of having a green house, you can make renovation changes to increase the green aspects of the house. This will appeal to a lot of potential buyers, and some of these strategies can save you money in the process.

What Does It Mean to Be Green?

There are two different organizations that can officially certify a house as being green. While they each have their own list of criteria, their lists share the same basic qualifications. A green home takes a variety of factors into account including the following:

- Where the house is located
- The design of the house
- The environmental impact of the house and its construction
- The materials used in construction
- The air quality inside the house
- An efficient use of water

Examples of Green Home Features

Green homes are built on land that does not negatively impact vital ecosystems like wetlands or the habitats of endangered species. They are relatively small, and are designed to get maximum exposure to natural light and air movement. Green homes are built with materials that are environmentally friendly in how they are made, what they are made of, how efficient they make the house, and how long they last.

A green home can also be one that was created out of something that already exists and would otherwise be discarded. For example, people have made homes out of old planes, old train cars, old buses, windmills, lighthouses, or other buildings such as churches, warehouses, and storefronts. Although these structures may not fit the definition of being certified green, they are creative reuses of material.

The house has windows and doors that are Energy Star rated, the heating, lighting, cooling, and water-heating systems are all energy efficient and all appliances are Energy Star rated. Green homes are water efficient, utilizing rain water wherever possible. Green homes also utilize the landscape to make the house more energy efficient by creating natural shading over the house.

Benefits of Including Green Technology in Your Renovations

A lot of the green home features listed aren't practical for a house flip. However, there are a wide range of renovation options that you can choose that will make the house more energy efficient and environmentally conscious. Choosing green renovations is good for the environment, but they are also good for resale. Potential buyers like the idea of having a green home, but they also like knowing their monthly utility bills will be lower because of the design of the house.

Recycling and Repurposing

Every renovation project should have a to-do list that is completed and prioritized with an attached wish list. You should also have a budget in mind; how much are you going to spend on your flip? Reusing old materials is always a good place to start. It is also environmentally friendly to reuse and repurpose materials. Additionally, recycling materials you can't reuse will have a positive impact on the environment.

Recycling

Almost everything can be recycled in some way. Recycling is defined as a process in which a given product is converted back to its base components and remade into a new product. Some untreated wood products, for example, can be turned into mulch or shredded to become engineered wood. If you are going to need mulch in the landscaping, you can make a pile of the wood you are pulling out of the house during demolition. When you are ready, you can rent a mulcher for a couple hours and create your own mulch. Since mulch can be quite expensive and equipment rental for a couple hours is not as expensive, you will likely save money doing it this way.

Just like aluminum cans and newspaper, there are materials during a demolition process that can be recycled. Sell whatever you cannot use in your renovation is some way. Some metals or pieces and parts can be sold to add a bit of money to your project. While it might sound like a lot of extra work, it really isn't if you're near a local scrapyard. Simply pull out the recyclable materials like metal siding, copper pipes, electrical wiring, gutters, etc., and load them into your truck. When everything is out, you can drive them right over to the scrapyard and collect payment. You don't have to do anything special to prepare the materials for the scrapyard, and you don't have to make an appointment to drop things off.

ESSENTIAL

Another recycled material that can be worked into the property is mulch made out of recycled car tires. This mulch lasts significantly longer and is softer than wood mulch—making it ideal for use around backyard playgrounds.

Repurposing

First and foremost, repurposing is not recycling. While they seem like the same thing, they are not. Unlike recycling, repurposing does not involve a breakdown process. More so, it is a conversion straight from one product into another making repurposed products cheaper. You get more bang for your buck, which is always a positive thing. During the demolition process, think about what you can reuse as you move into construction. For example, bricks can be reused if you chip off the old mortar. Unneeded trim or molding can be used in other areas of the house. A large piece of drywall salvaged from one room can be used to patch a hole in another room.

Repurposing is an excellent way to reduce your costs. Repurposed materials can come from your own demolition project, a junkyard, or a salvage retail store. There are different kinds of salvage retail stores. Some salvage stores collect materials from demolitions and sell them for dirt cheap. Other salvage stores buy second quality and overstock items from manufacturers and sell them for dirt cheap, too. Either way, you can save huge amounts of money, and you are being more environmentally friendly in the process. While prospective buyers may not be able to see all the ways you conserved material, you can promote the overall effort to be green during renovations.

Eco-Friendly Exteriors

Exterior cladding is the final surface on a house. Its main function is to protect the interior from the weather. When you think about cladding, your mind probably jumps to vinyl, engineered wood, aluminum, or masonry. There are alternatives available. While you were doing your research on recycled and repurposed materials locally available in your area, you probably found some exterior cladding alternatives.

Some materials used today contain hazardous chemicals like formaldehyde, as is the case with some engineered wood. Some masonry is harvested from the earth using explosives which devastates entire ecosystems. Always look into materials before committing to one to make sure you are being environmentally friendly.

Forest Stewardship Council (FSC) Certified Wood

Traditionally, wood siding has been seen as a green option because wood is a renewable resource. However, old growth forests are rapidly depleting because the wood is being harvested faster than it can regrow. For that reason, simply choosing wood is no longer enough to be green. The wood you choose has to be certified by the Forest Stewardship Council (FSC). This certification means that the company harvesting the wood is actively replanting forests as quickly as they are harvesting. They are creating a renewable resource by ensuring the forests have an opportunity to regrow. While there is a little more to the certification than that, replanting is the significant part.

QUESTION

Besides FSC wood, what other options are considered green?
Bamboo is a great alternative. It is hard, durable, and with a seven-year growth cycle, it is considered a highly renewable resource.

Fiber-Cement Siding

Fiber-cement siding has become a popular choice in green homes. It is made from a mixture of sand, cellulose fibers, cement, and other materials. It is fire-resistant, rot-resistant, termite-resistant, and it will not warp. It can be created to look like wood siding, vertical siding, or shingles. Additionally, it is warranted for fifty years and can last well beyond that. Fiber-cement siding is really the best option in regard to green exterior cladding.

Roofing and Solar Panels

Roofing is a tough subject to approach. A new roof is a dramatic improvement to any house. When selecting a material, look at the life cycle costs and short-term costs. Life cycle costs look into the durability and longevity of the material. How long until it needs to be replaced? Short-term costs are your upfront installation costs.

Synthetic Slate

Synthetic slate can be made out of a range of materials. Some synthetic slate is made from ground natural slate, resin, and fiberglass. Other synthetic slates are made from recycled rubber automobile tire threads. Overall, synthetic slate provides the appearance and durability of natural slate, but it is lighter and less likely to break. Additionally, it is being marketed as lasting forty to sixty years or even longer.

Metal Shingles

Metal shingles or panels can be made out of a variety of materials including aluminum, steel, or copper. They are lightweight, highly durable, fire-resistant, and long-lasting. They have a low environmental impact and they can last significantly longer than other roofing options. They can also be made to look like tile, slate, or wood shake, which allows people to have the look they want in an environmentally friendly way.

Solar Panels

Solar panels are a great addition to any house. There are a lot of different options today and there will be more as time progresses. Research is pushing the efficiency of solar panels up and the costs of them down. Right now the highest efficiency available on the market is about 19.7 percent. In the labs, the highest recorded efficiency is about 44.5 percent. The efficiency as a percent is a measure of how much solar energy is converted into electricity for the house.

With enough solar panels, your renovation can become a net-zero building. Net-zero is defined as a project that generates the electricity it requires to satisfy its demand, or the energy required. The energy required fluctuates as the months go by and the weather changes. The net required is satisfied by the net production. Add more panels and you can push into energy plus production status. Energy plus means your project generates more electricity than it demands.

FACT

Make sure your project is grid connected so the excess electricity can be sold back to the grid. Instead of paying bills on the house, your future buyers will get a check from the power grid. This will be a strong selling point for your flipped house.

HVAC

As mentioned in early sections, HVAC stands for heating, ventilation, and air conditioning. Like roofs, this is a big eco-friendly topic with lots of options available. Since you are trying to make your project eco-friendly, your search for an HVAC solution starts with your passive options. Passive systems run themselves for no energy cost to you or your future buyer.

Ventilation: Passive and Active

Ventilation is how a space gets fresh air. It is a very necessary function in a house, otherwise the air will get stale and uncomfortable. A byproduct of ventilation is cooling. For example, a fan can ventilate a room, but it also cools the room. The two kinds of passive ventilation are cross ventilation and stacked ventilation. Cross ventilation uses two openings, either windows or doors, to run a current of air through the house. Stacked ventilation, like what you get with a ceiling fan, uses a process by which hot air rises and cold air sinks to circulate air.

Passive ventilation might not be a good option for your project. Surrounding structures can limit air flow or your projects climate region might be low in wind current. If passive is not a viable option, there is simple and cheap active ventilation: fans. Fans create air currents that circulate air and freshen it. A fan in each space can improve air conditions dramatically. This can be as simple as installing ceiling fans throughout the house.

Heating and Cooling

Heating and cooling should be reserved for the extremes in your climate condition. Passive options are available depending on what climate your project is in. For example, a passive cooling strategy that works in Houston, Texas, will probably not work in Detroit, Michigan. Researching passive cooling strategies that will work for your specific area will allow you to save money while increasing the perceived value of the house.

ESSENTIAL

Use combinations of those three passive heating methods for higher performance in your project. You would be surprised how easily you can heat a whole house without the use of a heater.

Passive heating is done by direct sunlight, sunrooms, and/or thermal mass. Direct sunlight is created when sunlight hits windows and comes into the house as infrared energy or heat. Windows on the southern face of the house should be exposed to catch winter sun, but shielded to block summer sun through trees or awnings. Sunrooms are dedicated spaces that can be opened up to the rest of the house or closed off and opened up. Typically, they are all windows to generate the most heat possible. They can have a secondary use year-round. For example, you can have it function as a greenhouse and have your own garden year-round. Thermal mass are materials that when struck by sunlight, collect infrared energy and redistribute it to the adjacent room. Stone and masonry work well.

Active Systems

If passive systems are not for you, then an active system will be your next subject for research. There are a few different kinds of systems you can apply. Active systems are divided into two main categories: duct systems and ductless systems. Ducts are used to transport air. A ductless system takes up less space and, as the name implies, requires no ducts.

Duct Systems

You can run ducts above and/or below a space. How you run ducts varies based on how many floors your project has and what you want to accomplish for efficiency. One key point to remember with ducts is that they will leak. It does not matter what you do, they will leak. That is why you want your ducts within the condition space, or parts sealed up and insulated. Noninsulated space will lose heat in the winter and collect heat in the summer causing your duct efficiency to drop.

Typical houses are going to be one or two stories. One story houses give you the option of running your ducts under the floor or above the ceiling. If you want to run your ducts under the house, make sure your crawl space is big enough in case maintenance is required. Also, insulate and seal up your crawl space so the leaks in your ducts do not try to heat or cool a space connected directly to the outdoors. The same goes with ducts in the ceiling. Make sure you have attic access and that your attic is sealed up and insulated. Houses with two floors are very easy to solve with ducts. Running the ducts between the floors will keep your ducts within the conditioned space.

Duct systems are tied to large pieces of equipment for the heating and cooling of outside air to use within the house. There are two purposes to ducts: supply and return. Supply vents bring air into a space while return vents remove used air. A heat exchanger can be used to tie supply and return together and pass energy from one to another.

Ductless Systems

Ductless systems can either be separate units tied to a thermostat in each space or a series of units tied together with piping. Separate units are good to control the temperature in every space within the house. Smaller houses might only require a couple units while larger houses will require more units. They take in air and exchange heat with piping and then resupply the space.

Another option is radiator units. Radiators use radiation heat to supply hot air into a space. Piping with hot water runs through a metallic unit and heats the metal. The metal in turn passes the heat into the space.

Water Heating Systems

Hot water is important, but can also be a huge energy waste. Maintaining a hot water tank means endlessly heating several gallons of water to just sit there until it is needed. This is inefficient and can be very expensive depending on how your hot water tank is heated.

While hot water is used in showers and sinks, there is another use. In the previous section on HVAC, you learned about passive heating systems. Well, you can passively heat a house using your passively heated water. Running piping in your floor can allow you to re-radiate heat up into spaces. Heat wants to rise, so it starts in the floor at the occupants feet and goes up. This would allow you to heat the house without the strong dependence on gas or electricity.

QUESTION

Aren't there "green" water heaters, as opposed to alternative systems? You can choose to replace an older or outdated water heater with a certified Energy Star water heater. They can be found in both gas and electric.

Solar Water Heating

Solar water systems are becoming more popular in this century as homeowners want to save money on their monthly electric bill. A solar water heating system is actually pretty simple. Piping runs in a loop between a heat exchanger and your roof. In the roof, it runs back and forth to collect heat from a re-radiation of solar energy through the roof cladding. The heat exchanger passes the heat from the roof loop to a house loop. The house loop connects the heat exchanger to the hot water storage unit. The hot water storage then supplies your shower and sinks.

Geothermal Water

An alternative to solar water is geothermal water. A geothermal system runs two loops tied between a heat exchanger just like the solar water system except for one critical detail: the heat collector loop runs down into the earth. It is easier to apply this method on new construction, but it is still possible to apply to a renovation project.

Tankless Water Heaters

Tankless water heaters are beneficial because, as the name suggests, there is no need to keep 40 or 50 gallons of water hot at all times. There are tankless water heaters that can heat water for an entire house or there are point of use water heaters. For example, if you primarily want hot water to go to the kitchen, you can install a point of use tankless water heater under the kitchen sink, and it will heat water as needed.

Green Flooring Options

Flooring can be a big issue when renovating a house. A lot of the mainstream flooring options are not considered green because of how they are produced, as well as their relatively short life span. There are green options with almost all types of floors including wood floors, carpeted floors, and linoleum floors. While green flooring can be significantly more expensive, you can use it in a smaller area of the house that will have a big impact on the perceived value. That way, you get the positive impact of choosing a green option without the enormous expense of installing it throughout the entire house.

FSC Hardwood

This is the same wood you can choose to use in exterior cladding and other areas of the house. It is hardwood that was harvested responsibly by companies committed to an environmentally conscious mission. You can get almost any hardwood FSC certified. Additionally, since the consumer is willing to pay more for green flooring, the manufacturers of this type of flooring also often use nontoxic adhesives and finishes to extend the beneficial nature of the product.

Bamboo

Bamboo is a great material to use for flooring. It is very hard and durable. It is not porous, which makes it easier to clean, and it is relatively inexpensive. Bamboo is harvested from the bamboo plant. It is considered a green flooring option because the bamboo plant only has a seven-year growing cycle.

Bamboo has proven to be very useful in several different applications. It can be used for exterior cladding, flooring, counters, and cabinets, as well as serving dishes and utensils.

Cork

Cork flooring is made from the bark of a cork oak tree. When harvested correctly, the tree is not damaged. It is renewable and environmentally friendly. It has both thermal and acoustic qualities. It is also fire-resistant, insect-resistant, lightweight, durable, and warm to the touch. Cork flooring can last for eight to ten years before needing replacement. You can buy cork flooring in large tiles, which are easy to install.

Marmoleum

Marmoleum is a natural linoleum. It is bio-based, nontoxic, and antimicrobial. It is very easy to clean and maintain, which makes it perfect for kitchens and bathrooms. It is also very durable and has a long life span, which means it won't have to be replaced every couple years.

Wool Carpet

Wool has been woven and used in rugs for centuries. Yet, most of today's carpeting is made from synthetic fibers that go through a great deal of chemical processing during production. Wool carpeting is very durable, thick, and warm. It is also made from a renewable resource that doesn't harm the animals or the environment. Wool carpeting is going to be solidly more expensive than a cheaper alternative. However, the look and feel of the carpeting is significantly better. If installed in a strategic location, you can reap the benefits without having to spend a lot.

Other Green Renovation Options

Water conservation, lighting, and energy conservation are also important factors when describing a house as being green. These factors are important because they deal with the consumption of water, light, and heat. Conserving these elements where possible will decrease usage, which will decrease monthly expenses. Once again, you want to appeal to prospective buyers through both the environmental efforts, as well as the cost savings to them.

Water Conservation

A simple and inexpensive way to promote water conservation is by installing a rain barrel in the back of the house. This is a way to collect rain water for use in nonconsumption ways. For example, rain water can be collected and used to water the garden, wash the dog, or fill a kiddie pool. The cost of setting up a rain collection system is minimal, yet the benefits are lasting. Additionally, the upkeep and care of rain storage systems is minimal, so prospective buyers will be able to focus on the benefits.

Lighting

Natural lighting is very important in green homes. You can add natural lighting by increasing the number of windows in the house. You can also add skylights, where possible. Where you can't add natural lighting, you can add LED lighting, which utilizes minimal wattage yet provides better lighting. You can also install motion switches with the lighting, so lights go off automatically when people leave the room.

Windows

Windows are a significant source of heat loss in a house. In order to decrease heat loss, you can replace the windows with double pane windows or you can improve the existing windows. One way to improve existing windows is by weather-sealing them. Additionally, having properly fitting and working storm windows and window screens will allow homeowners to better utilize the windows for light and temperature control.

ESSENTIAL

Simply making sure there are screens in all the windows will allow homeowners to open their windows, a natural way to control temperature during certain times of the year.

Sorting Through Your Options

This chapter has covered a wide range of green renovation options. However, you have to decide which options will actually work for the house you are renovating, which renovations are cost effective, and which renovations will increase the perceived value of the house the most. The easiest place to start will be deciding which renovations are even possible for the house you are working on. For example, if the house has a perfectly good water heater, you can eliminate water heating options. There is no point or benefit to replacing a perfectly good water heater. Once you weed out all the green renovations that just aren't practical, you can move on to decide which ones are the most cost-effective.

Deciding Which Renovations Are Worth the Money

The next step is to decide which green renovation options will be cost effective. While many green options will be more expensive than their non-green counterparts, you need to decide if the difference in price is worth the payoff in the end. This refers to your return on investment (ROI). This means the money you spend on a specific renovation increases the actual value of the house and your ability to increase the asking price or the ability to sell the house faster. For example, a new metal front door has proven to have more than a 70 percent ROI. That means if you have an older front door on the house, it is worth the investment to buy a new door.

Go through your remaining list of possible renovations and see what the price difference would be for you to choose a green option. Then decide how the renovation would improve the perceived value of the house. For example, the solar panels would drastically decrease the electrical costs of the house to the extent that the homeowners might even get paid to have them there. This can be a major selling point. As you go through your list cross off the ones that are either too expensive or the increase in perceived value isn't enough.

Getting the Most Impact Out of Your Renovations

By now, you should have the short list of possible green renovations. Try to do as many as you can in order to really promote the green features of the house. For some renovations, you may not be able to complete the renovation for the entire house. For example, you might love the high-end look of bamboo floors, but they aren't financially practical to install throughout the entire house. Instead of scrapping the idea altogether decide where bamboo floors might have the greatest impact. In this situation, the answer is probably going to be the kitchen.

Likewise, if you can't afford to put LED lighting throughout the entire house because of the cost, focus on the bathrooms. You'll get the biggest impact in those rooms. You can strategically include green renovations to enhance the overall look and perceived value of the home. Along the same lines, you wouldn't want to spend the money putting all natural wool carpeting in closets where no one will really see it or walk on it.

CHAPTER 12

Working with a Realtor

There are many advantages to working with a realtor, but there are also a few disadvantages. While the role of a realtor is one you can do yourself, having a realtor do it for you provides you with a multitude of resources that you otherwise wouldn't have. When first starting out, working with a realtor will save you from the inevitable mistakes of the learning curve.

Understanding the Selling Process

Working with a realtor will make selling your house much easier for you. They will walk you through the process, do a majority of the work, and provide you with access to their professional resources and networks. That being said, understanding the selling process and everything they do will help you to better appreciate their role and effort in the flipping process. Many people see paying a realtor as an unneeded expense, and for those that have the know-how and resources, it may indeed be an unneeded expense. However, for the majority of new house flippers, it is a very necessary expense.

Setting a Price

The first thing your realtor will be doing is determining a selling price range for the house. This process involves touring the house and taking notes regarding the features of the house including size, number of bedrooms, number of bathrooms, and extra selling features such as a porch, central air, outdoor storage, etc. The realtor will take all this information and then look at comparables in the area.

The realtor is trained to identify which properties in the area are really comparable to the house you are selling. Being a comparable property means more than being the same approximate size or having the same number of bedrooms. Comparables cover a wide range of features. In some cases, it is difficult to find true comparables. In these situations, your realtor will rely on what information is available to her, along with what she knows about the market and what features influence the selling price. For example, regardless of neighborhood, brick houses sell for more than non-brick houses and corner lots sell for more than noncorner lots. These are the kinds of features your realtor will take into account when suggesting a price for your house.

Stage the House

Once a price is set, the target market for the house will have already been identified. The realtor will then work with you to stage the house in a way that will appeal to the target market. Many realtors may already have the furniture and accessories to stage the house themselves, or they may have a professional stager on their team of people. Either way, the realtor will ensure the house is staged in a way that will appeal to prospective buyers, highlight the house's more desirable features, and give the impression of spacious, low-maintenance living.

ESSENTIAL

Make sure the pictures are not taken until after the house has been staged. This will make your marketing material stronger and more enticing.

Once the house is clean and staged, the realtor will walk through the house and around the property taking pictures of everything. These pictures will be used in the marketing material for the house. The realtor may also choose to create a video tour of the house to post online, if doing so is one of her normal marketing tactics. Either way, your realtor will work to create images of the house that will be both appealing and enticing. The goal of posting images and videos online is to get people to want to visit the property.

Market the House

Your realtor will then start marketing your house. She will get the house on the Multiple Listing Service (MLS), which allows all other realtors in the area to see the house. This is beneficial because it allows other realtors to also market your house if they have clients looking in the area and your house fits their criteria. Your realtor will also use the pictures she took to create fliers and fact sheets. She will write descriptions of the house for prospective buyers. She will also promote the house through her company's online and offline channels.

Arrange an Open House and Showings

Your realtor will schedule an open house, which is an opportunity for prospective buyers to come look at the house and ask any questions they may have about the house. Open houses are generally two-hour events. The realtor will also arrange showings with interested prospective buyers and other realtors that have prospective buyers. Your realtor will stay available with little notice to show the house when the opportunity arises. Since you don't live in the house, this will be zero-stress or frustration for you.

Targeting Your Market

When trying to sell a house, there are two markets you need to consider: the housing market and your target market. Your target market are the buyers that are most likely to want to buy your house based on size, location, and price. Your realtor will have a solid understanding of both, and additionally what you need to do in order to sell your house quickly. There are strategies for both dealing with the housing market and the target market in a productive way.

Target the Housing Market

The housing market will not only dictate how you are able to price your house, but also how you need to approach negotiations. Once the price is set, and you start getting offers, your realtor can help you go through each offer to decide which is the best option for you. Your realtor will also be able to help you decide when you should counter and when you should accept the offer on the table. Based on his understanding of the market, your realtor will have a pretty good idea of how much you can realistically get for the house.

Target Your Potential Buyers

Targeting potential buyers is also important when setting the price and staging the home. For example, if you are selling a house with three or more bedrooms in a good school district with a good size yard, you can assume you will have people with families looking at the house. With that in mind, you can stage at least one of the bedrooms to be a kids' bedroom, as opposed to a home office or guest room. Additionally, while showing the house, your realtor can point out the school system, the house's proximity to parks, and other kid attractions.

ALERT

If you don't know who your target market is, you won't be able to effectively stage and market the house. Understanding the target market is the cornerstone of all marketing.

The Cost of a Realtor

A realtor is paid a predetermined commission of the house sale. When you hire a realtor to sell a house for you, you will sign a contract with that realtor. This will prevent you from cutting the realtor out of the deal by selling the house yourself. If you do make a connection and find a buyer on your own, your realtor will still get his percentage of the sale. Although it is highly beneficial to help sell your house, you shouldn't go into it thinking that you can save money if you find the buyer. This contract also prevents you from working with another realtor without giving your first realtor a genuine opportunity to sell the house.

What Benefits Come with That Cost

A good realtor will bring a great deal of benefits to the table. Like any salesperson, realtors understand that they are only paid if they sell the houses, so they are highly motivated to sell and sell quickly. A qualified realtor will have years of training and experience behind him. Realtors will have the resources to provide all your needed marketing materials, which will save you a great deal of money. They also provide exposure to a wider market. They have the backing and name recognition of the realty company they are working for, which depending on the company, can be enormous.

Regardless of what realty company they work for, there are good realtors and bad realtors, just as there are experienced realtors and inexperienced realtors. In order to get the full benefits and make the money you pay worth it, it is essential that you find a qualified realtor with the experience and track record to help you accomplish your goals.

When and How Are Realtor's Costs Covered?

Realtor costs aren't covered until the house sells, which is a positive. If you are paying the realtor fees, they can come out of the profit you make off the house. However, realtor fees are also negotiable closing costs with the buyer. All closing costs can be negotiated individually or as a group. Depending on what kind of sale arrangement you make with the buyer, the realtor fees may be covered by them. However, if they aren't, you will need to pay them upon closing.

Realtors are paid on a percentage. Generally speaking, it is a low percentage, around 3 percent of the selling price. Realtors have to sell a lot of houses to make a good amount of money, which is why the good ones are highly motivated. When looking for a realtor, it is good to find one that is selling real estate full-time. A lot of people sell real estate on the side because the nature of the job provides that flexibility. However, you want to work with someone that is fully committed to the job.

Closing Costs to Consider

There are a number of closing costs to consider when selling a house. As previously mentioned, closing costs can be negotiated with the buyer. Not that you can negotiate the amount of the closing costs, but you can negotiate who pays them. One of the best strategies to getting buyers to agree to the closing costs is by accepting their offer with the condition that they cover closing costs. As long as their offer is a reasonable one, this will give you a quick sale with no additional costs, and it will leave the buyer feeling like she got a great deal. Although closing costs can vary from one house to another, there are some basic closing costs that will be present with nearly all house sales.

QUESTION

Is there a way to sell a property without closing costs?
No. Closing costs are one of the many costs of doing business that you will need to accept. Although you can always try to negotiate the buyers paying the closing costs, if they refuse, you either have to pay them or walk away from the sale.

Realtor Fees

The realtor fee, as discussed earlier, is a small percentage of the sale price. Both the buyer and seller may be working with a realtor. Depending on the selling price, this may actually be a significant fee. You can group this in with total closing costs when negotiating or you can individualize your closing costs. You can specifically ask that the buyer pay the realtor fees, or you can offer to pay your own realtor fees under the condition that the buyer pays all the other closing costs. There are a number of ways to approach negotiating closing costs, and your realtor can help you with that.

Inspection and Appraisal Costs

Unless you are working with an FHA loan, you can negotiate who pays for the inspection and appraisal. In most cases, these fees are picked up by the buyer because they are in the interest of the buyer. You can assert that if buyers want an inspection on the house, they need to pay for it. Same goes for the appraisal; while an appraisal might be required depending on where you live, it is also in the interest of the buyer. You, as the seller, can agree to allow the inspector and appraiser onto your property, as long as the buyer pays the fees. These are usually flat rates. Although it will vary by area, inspections and appraisals generally cost a few hundred dollars each.

Title Transfer Fees

The title transfer fee is the fee paid to the title company for legally transferring the title from the seller to the buyer. This is also paid at the time of closing, and can be negotiated between the buyer and seller. Title transfer fees are dependent on where you live, so it is important to look into those before negotiating cost and terms. Unlike realtors or inspections, there is no way around title transfer fees. You cannot sell a house without the work of a title company, so this is a definite fee.

Bank Fees

If the buyer is working with a bank to buy the house, there may also be bank fees. This is another fee due at closing in order for the house to be legally transferred. This is a fee commonly paid by the buyer, opposed to the seller. However, it should be discussed while negotiating terms of the contract. The amount owed in bank fees will depend on the bank and the selling price of the house, so they can vary dramatically. Bank fees are only a concern if the bank is involved with the transfer of the house.

Evaluating Offers

When selling a house, you set the asking price at the amount you want to get based on the research your realtor did on comparables and house value. This is referred to as the asking price because it is what you are asking people to pay for the house. The asking price opens the door for negotiations because it lets prospective buyers know your ideal number. This prevents having to entertain offers that are nowhere near what you would be willing to accept for the house.

When a prospective buyer is interested, he can make an offer on the house. The initial offer may include the price he is offering to pay, as well as the terms he is willing to agree to. For example, a buyer could offer to pay your asking price if you agree to cover all the closing costs. Or along the same lines, the buyer could offer a price a few thousand dollars less than what you are asking, but offer to cover the closing costs. Some buyers will intentionally put in a low offer just to see your response. When negotiating, one side tends to go high while the other side tends to go low because each is hoping to get the upper hand in the negotiation. By making a low offer, the buyer is giving you the opportunity to counteroffer.

ESSENTIAL

Don't wait too long to make a counteroffer. Just as you don't like to be left waiting, neither do other people. If you wait too long, the prospective buyer may be less likely to negotiate with you.

Making Counteroffers

A counteroffer is your official response to the offers you receive. A counteroffer can offer a different price, terms, or both. You are under no obligation to accept any offer or any terms of an offer. However, it is better to make a counteroffer than to just say no. This gives the prospective buyer the opportunity to decide what he is really willing to pay for the house. Generally speaking, the negotiations don't go too far past the counteroffer or a counteroffer from the buyer in response to the seller's counteroffer. In large deals with many terms, the negotiations may go on for weeks. However, in most cases, it only takes a couple of days to either come to an agreement or walk away.

Allowing Your Realtor to be the Middleman

When working with a realtor, it is important to let the realtor be your middleman. Don't contact a buyer directly to discuss the terms of an offer or counteroffer. Your realtor should come to you with the offer presented by the prospective buyer. You will let your realtor know what your counteroffer is or if you are willing to accept the offer. Your realtor will contact the buyer's realtor and it goes forward from there. Letting your realtor be the middleman accomplishes a couple of things. First, it allows you to sell the houses without the stress of also having to communicate with prospective buyers. Secondly, it allows emotion to stay out of the negotiations. If you are negotiating directly with a prospective buyer, there is no filter for emotional responses, dirty looks, waivering, etc. Your realtor just provides you with the facts of the offer and relays your messages accurately.

It is, however, important to understand that a realtor cannot negotiate on your behalf. Her job is to relay messages, and when an offer is accepted, she processes the sale. If you have a lawyer acting as your sales representative, a lawyer would have the ability to negotiate on your behalf, but a realtor will not.

Coming to an Agreement

A sales agreement is met when both you and the prospective buyer agree on a price and terms. Once this is accomplished, you and the buyer will enter into a contract. At that time, the buyer may put down earnest money. This is to hold the contract. Basically, entering into a contract means you are agreeing not to entertain any more offers for a period of time, which gives the buyers the opportunity to arrange their home loan to be processed. Once this is taken care of, everything will go to the title company and a closing date will be set. The closing date is the date all the papers are signed and the keys are given to the new homeowner.

If the time limit of the contract expires and the prospective buyer has still not arranged the funding to buy the house, the contract is void. You can then accept other offers, put the house back on the market, etc. The prospective buyers do not get their earnest money back. Think of this as a deposit you lose when you don't return something on time.

Having a Plan B

While selling your house quickly is ideal, that doesn't always happen. There are a wide range of reasons a house may not sell at a particular time or at a particular price. It is important to have a Plan B so that your investment isn't completely lost. You have a couple of options. The first is to reduce the price of the house. While this cuts directly into your profits, if the price is lower, the house will sell, and you may be better off in the long-run taking the hit. Talk to your realtor to determine why the house may not be selling.

ALERT

Not having a Plan B is setting yourself up for disaster. Regardless of how well you stage or market the property, not all properties sell right away.

Selling to a Property Investor

Most realtors work primarily with the general public buying homes to live in. However, there are also other property investors, who actively buy up properties in their preferred areas to rent out. While they are making a significant investment up front, this provides them with long-term monthly income. You can seek out landlords to see if they would be interested in buying the house. When talking to landlords, you need to focus on the features of the property that will allow them to maximize their potential profits by increasing the amount they can charge for rent.

A good place to start if you are interested in working with property investors is professional landlord organizations. If you do not have an organization in your area that has actual meetings, you can go online and look for online property investor forums and communities. It is good to network and develop relationships with other property investors as soon as you get into the business. If you are already on close terms with some investors, it won't be a big deal to contact them and let them know what you have available.

Renting the Property

Many house flippers will rent houses they are unable to sell within a certain period of time. Renting the house will cover the monthly costs and provide a monthly profit while still trying to sell the house. You can rent the property until you find a better solution, or you can choose to keep the property as a rental for a longer period of time. Holding onto the property for at least a year will also allow you to only pay long-term capital gains tax when you do sell the property, which will save you money in the long run.

This approach has both advantages and disadvantages. The advantages include money coming in monthly instead of going out. The house will be occupied, which will make it less likely to be vandalized. Additionally, the tenants will be taking care of things like mowing the lawn so you won't have to spend the man hours on property upkeep. The disadvantages, however, are fairly substantial. Once you start renting a house, selling it to a homeowner will become increasingly more difficult. At that point, you need to look at selling it to a property investor, if you aren't already.

Selling on Land Contract

Another Plan B option may be to consider a creative selling plan such as a land contract. These are for people interested in buying, who cannot buy at the moment, but will be able to buy in the foreseeable future. A land contract is a legal agreement that the occupants will rent the house for a period of time. Then, at the end of that predetermined time, they will buy the house. As long as they go through with the purchase, the money they paid in rent will go toward the purchase of the house. If they do not go through with the purchase, you keep the money they already paid as rent, and they have no equity in the house.

CHAPTER 13

Selling Without a Realtor

Selling without a realtor is perfectly legal and acceptable in many situations. The role of a realtor is to act as a liaison between you and other parties (both buyers and sellers) as well as to ensure the entire process goes smoothly. With the right understanding of the business, you can take on the role of realtor for your transactions. You can also choose to work with a lawyer, which might be a clear option depending on your situation.

Know the Risks Before You Sell

Before deciding to sell without a realtor, it is important to know what you will be getting into. There are risks involved in working without a realtor. While most of these risks can be mitigated to an extent, they are still there, and overcoming them will take additional time, work, and resources.

While working without a realtor will save money on paper, the reality of the situation may be different. Until you have a solid support network set up and you've gained some experience in the process of buying and selling, a realtor can save you time and money. However, understanding the risks and being prepared for them can allow you to overcome them and be successful without the aid of a realtor.

Lack of Exposure

Realtors have an already established marketing network. They have the availability of signs, cards, fliers, and name recognition. When going through a realtor, your house may be included in full-color newspaper ads, home selling magazines, and on the company's website. They have years of experience and work behind their efforts. This isn't something you can grow overnight. In order to compete with the exposure of a realtor, you will need to work hard to get your house visible to the public. You'll also have to work on growing your own network of contacts and resources, so that marketing a house will become easier as you go.

FACT

Part of a realtor's exposure is name recognition. If they work for a big realty company, there is a level of trust and assurance already assumed by potential buyers. Realtors get to work off the reputation of their company.

Lack of Resources

Realtors have a wide range of resources at their disposal. They have the resources of their office, which includes signs, copy services, web support, and more. You will need to consider all the things a realtor generally provides, and you will need to make arrangements and considerations to provide those things yourself. This can be more expensive at first. For example, having your own signs made will be a significant upfront expense. However, once they are made, you have them at your disposal. There are a wide range of companies that can make signs for you, so you can shop around for the best price. You can also research the long-term price difference of buying your own color copier or paying to have copies made with each house.

Lack of Experience

Realtors also come with training and experience. They already have an understanding of the applicable laws and taxes that you need to know about. They know what disclosures you need to provide, and they know how to create copy and talk to people in a way that will sell houses. All of this can be learned. It might take you some time, but all of this can be learned. You may choose to use a realtor on your first couple sales, and then handle it on your own. You may also choose to go through realtor training. This will provide you with the same background information at your realtor's disposal.

Learning How to Set a Price

Without a realtor, you will need to learn how to set the asking price of the house. To do this, you need to see what other houses are selling for in your area. You also need to research how specific features affect the asking price. For example, can you ask more because the house has an in-ground pool or a finished basement?

Identifying Comparables

Comparables have been discussed several times. However, when doing this on your own for the first time, you may have trouble identifying what exactly the comparables are for your house. Start by getting a list of houses that are for sale in your area. Then go through and find the houses that are approximately similar—same number of bedrooms, bathrooms, and amenities. Although you won't find houses exactly like yours, you want to look at houses that have many of the same general characteristics.

Once you've identified the comparables in your area, you can look at the price they are selling at. If there is a considerable difference in asking price between two houses you have identified as comparables, you will need to go back to those two houses and try to see what accounts for the difference in price and then figure out which house is more similar to your house. Once you have a few comparables that are all in a similar price range, you will be able to set an asking price for your house. Don't be afraid to go a little on the high side of your chosen range. This will leave room for negotiations.

Doing Online Market Research

Another thing you can do to help set the asking price of your house is online research of your market area. Look at the tax values of houses in your area. Look at the schools and where the parks are located. These can all be selling points that you should know about. Also, you should know approximately how close the house is to major highways, hospitals, and more. Knowing this ahead of time will allow you to quickly and effectively answer questions from prospective buyers. You can also use some of this information in your marketing of the house. For example, if the house is located on the same street as a major park, you can describe it as "steps away from xyz park."

QUESTION

What if I do everything in my power to market the house and don't receive any response to my first open house?
Get help from someone with concrete local marketing experience, and then plan a second open house. Don't wait a few weeks, get started right away.

The Importance of Marketing

You cannot sell a house by simply putting out a sign and hoping for the best. If you are working without a realtor, you will need to go the extra mile to market the house yourself. You won't have the same exposure or connections realtors do, so you are going to have be creative and work hard to get the information out there. Marketing is essential and the sooner you start the better response you are going to get. Don't be afraid to create fliers and post them in high-traffic areas. Advertise your open house on Craigslist, Backpages, and every other online classified ad or forum you can find.

Marketing Your House on Your Own

When selling a house yourself, you will have to create all your own marketing material. While this doesn't need to be overly expensive, it can be time-consuming. Give yourself plenty of time to take and edit the photos, write descriptions, and create ads. You will also need to do the leg work yourself. This includes making the copies, calling the papers, and arranging for ads to be published in prominent places. Marketing a house effectively is a big job, and if you are not working with a realtor, you may need help just getting everything done.

Getting the Exposure You'll Need to Attract Buyers

In order to get the exposure you are going to need to find a buyer, you will have to create a multimedia campaign. Focus on newspapers, online, and word-of-mouth. If you've made connections within the real estate market or with other property investors, ask them to help you promote the house through their channels as well. There are also marketing opportunities through For Sale By Owner (FSBO) service companies. These are companies dedicated to helping people get some of the same advantages they would have if they were working with a realtor. While you do have to pay for these services, depending on the asking price of the house, it may be the more cost effective option.

Working with Landlords and Other Property Investors

Another option is to market houses before you even buy them to renovate. This is taking a completely different approach to house flipping, and it means dealing specifically with other property investors. You may make less per flip taking this approach, but you will be able to make more deals faster. This approach might be best explained through a real life example.

Russ Harkins flipped houses for nearly twenty years. During that time, he developed a method that allowed him to flip many houses quickly without risk of the house not selling. He joined forces with a group of local investors who were only interested in buying single-family homes to manage as rentals. Russ Harkins would find houses that needed to be renovated and show them to these investors. They would pick out the houses they were interested in buying, and they would agree on a selling price before Russ even bought the house. This allowed him to know exactly how much room he had to make renovations and still turn a profit.

He would then buy the house and make all the needed renovations. Because the house was going to be used for a rental and he knew what kinds of things the investors were looking for, he was able to save money by renovating the house the way they wanted as opposed to how he might renovate it to attract prospective buyers. When he was done with the renovations, he would call the investors back and they would start the paperwork to buy the house. This arrangement saved him the time and energy of staging, marketing, and selling the house. It saved him the expense of using a realtor, and it also allowed him to immediately move on to the next flip.

Networking Opportunities

Always take advantage of networking opportunities. When there are meetings, conferences, and other types of outings where a group of property investors are gathered together, this is the perfect opportunity to network and make connections that will help you sell properties. The important part of these types of events is the socializing time. People don't make deals during a conference. They make deals at the bar that evening. Likewise, deals are not made during informational meetings and presentations; they are made while socializing over coffee after the meeting.

FACT

The Lake Erie Landlord Association plans casino bus trips. A bunch of members and their spouses will travel a few hours by bus to spend the day at the casino. While these are marketed as fun social day trips, the actual bus trip is often spent buying and selling properties between members. It gives them a few hours to sit together and work out details.

Understanding What They Are Looking For

This will vary depending on where your house is located. However, generally speaking, landlords want things that are uniform. Instead of painting each room a different color, they paint the entire interior of a house one color. This makes it easier to touch up and repaint when tenants move out. A lot of landlords also prefer hard floors over carpeting because it is easier to clean and cheaper to replace. However, these are generalities. If you are interested in working with property investors to try to sell your houses as rentals, the best thing you can do is talk to local investors. See if anyone is interested in the opportunity, and if you find some investors that are, ask them what general things they do or look for when fixing up a rental property.

How to Sell a House Step-by-Step

How to sell a house has been discussed in terms of what your realtor will be doing and what you can do to help. However, if you are selling the house without a realtor, you will need to have a solid understanding of the process and exactly what you need to be doing to make the sale happen.

Setting a Price

As discussed earlier, you will need to learn how to set the asking price. The asking price needs to be competitive with the other available houses on the market. Once you decide on an asking price, you will need to include it with all your marketing materials.

Staging

Staging will start with cleaning the house and bringing in and arranging furniture. Trying to sell an empty house is not a good idea. Even though it might seem like being empty will make the house look larger, in reality, it makes it hard for prospective buyers to visualize their own stuff in the house.

Marketing

You will market the house both online and offline. You'll schedule an open house and market the open house as widely as you can. Following the open house, you will follow up with the people that attended and work to schedule follow-up appointments.

Negotiating a Contract

Once an offer is made on the house, you will start negotiating the contract. Without a realtor, you will be discussing the terms directly with the buyer's realtor in order to come to an agreement. Their realtor will not be able to negotiate on the buyer's behalf, so the negotiations may take a few days and several phone calls.

Closing the Deal

Once you come to an agreement with the terms and prices, you will need to enter a sales contract with the potential buyer. This will give the buyer time to get the loan they need to buy the house. Once a closing date is set, you can sign your papers and hand over the keys.

ALERT

It is important to remember that the house isn't sold until the papers are signed. While it might be exciting to get an offer on the house or even sign a contract, the sale can still fall through up until the title is transferred.

FSBO Services

FSBO (For Sale By Owner) services are professional services offered to individuals trying to sell a house without a realtor. They offer a wide range of services to make the selling process easier. An FSBO service company can help get your house listing on the same MLS list that realtors use. This will make your house searchable to real estate agents throughout the area, who are working with potential buyers to find homes.

FSBO service companies will help by offering you the opportunity to advertise your house in magazines and online. They offer real-estate lawyer services to help with whatever questions you may have. They can also provide you with disclosure and contract forms, as well as other sales documents you may need throughout the process. These are all things realtors have easy access to. Providing these forms to individuals minimizes the gap in risks.

FSBO service companies can also provide you with yard signs and weatherproof information boxes for fliers, if you choose to use them. While you do pay for these services, the amount you are going to pay will be competitive with what you would be paying to buy everything yourself, and going through a company will make getting everything you need fast and easy.

Finally, FSBO service companies also provide information booklets, materials, and seminars to help people learn how to sell houses. This is ideal if you plan to continue flipping houses; you can learn a great deal about the logistics of house selling, as well as tactics for marketing and staging. They will also teach you what type of information has to be disclosed in your state.

The Growth of FSBO Services

FSBO service companies grew out of a need for another option. While selling a house without a realtor has always been an option, individual sellers had no way to access many of the resources realtors had access to, putting them at a significant disadvantage. Many people felt they really didn't have a choice if they wanted to sell their house quickly.

The Advantages and Disadvantages of FSBO Services

The advantages of using FSBO services is that you get all the advantages of working with a realtor without having to work with a realtor. You have access to needed resources and information. You can also get training on how to better sell houses on your own. Additionally, you won't be locked into a contract with a realtor. For many, this is the most important aspect. Being stuck in a contract with a realtor that isn't doing the job, is both costly and frustrating.

Despite the clear benefits of utilizing these services, there are a couple of disadvantages. The first is the cost. Going with FSBO isn't exactly cost-effective. Although it depends on the selling price of your house, you may end up spending more trying to sell it yourself while working with an FSBO service company. Additionally, you don't get the same level of support you would get with a realtor. Although they are there to help, it is important to realize you will still be very much on your own.

CHAPTER 14

Preparing to Stage the House

Staging is an important step in selling a house. A lot of people associate staging with interior decorating, but it's really not the same at all. Staging is a combination of cleaning, decorating, and marketing. However, it is important to remember that it is mostly marketing. Staging should play up the house's positive features and play down the house's negative features. Staging a house can make people see it as a home, instead of just another house.

What Is Staging?

Staging is a process of emphasizing the house's positive features and maximizing the house's appeal to prospective buyers. Staging a house prior to a showing can increase the perceived value of the house and it can help you move the house more quickly.

"Staging" is actually a relatively new term coined in the mid-1980s, but realtors have been aware of the benefits of staging a house for years. The thoughts and ideas behind staging practices are a combination of interior design, marketing, and psychology. Understanding what buyers are looking for enables sellers to emphasize those things in the house.

QUESTION

Should I hire a professional stager?
While a professional stager can be very helpful, staging is a process you should learn anyway if you are going to be flipping many houses. Doing the research and accomplishing it yourself will help develop your base of knowledge and experience.

Why Is Staging Important?

Although what buyers are looking for may vary widely, there are certain buyer preferences that are almost universal. These are the preferences you want to play up when staging a house. For example, when given several options, buyers will show preference toward the house that appears to be the most spacious. This does *not* mean the largest house. It means the house that is perceived as the most spacious.

A lot of staging techniques are fairly common sense and some aren't exactly applicable when dealing with a flip. However, the idea behind them is important to understand. The majority of people are unable to visualize the potential in a space. Additionally, the majority of people cannot see past a mess or clutter.

According to StagedHomes.com, staged homes sell for 6.9 percent more than nonstaged homes. Additionally, staged homes are on the market for an average of eleven days less than nonstaged homes. While staging may require spending some money upfront, you have to think of it as an investment that you will see a return on.

The Staging Process

When flipping a house, the staging process actually starts while you are still working on renovations. It starts with choosing the wall colors, installing proper lighting, installing new floors, and repainting trim and ceilings. Essentially, all the cosmetic renovations you make are a part of the staging process.

Once the house is fully renovated, the next step is cleaning. Presenting the house as perfectly clean is an essential part of staging. Common sense dictates that houses require regular cleaning in order to stay nice. However, presenting a dirty, dusty house will only remind prospective buyers how much they hate cleaning. When you present a clean house, you give prospective buyers the impression that the house is easy to maintain, this will draw them in.

Finally, once the house is renovated and clean, you have to strategically decorate the rooms. Research has shown that most people are unable to visualize the potential in the room. For this reason, you need to help them along. This includes strategically placing furniture in the house so prospective buyers can see where furniture might look nice. Accessories like wall clocks, scenic pictures, vases, and fresh flowers will make the house feel inviting. Strategically placing furniture and accessories can also work to make rooms look larger and more spacious. It will also make the house seem easy to keep organized.

ESSENTIAL

The term "strategically" is used because how you decorate and where you place furniture is very important. As mentioned, staging is psychological, so you want to entice specific thoughts and responses from prospective buyers. Don't just throw in some furniture and hope for the best.

Doing Your Research

If you aren't sure how to decorate the house strategically, the best thing you can do is some research. Research other houses in the area, as well as home décor magazines. Regardless of what you decide to do, it is also important to remember to keep it simple. When it comes to staging, less is more.

Understanding the Influence of the Asking Price

It is important to research the comparables for the house you are flipping. How you stage a $90,000 house and a $250,000 will be different because the expectations of the buyers will be different. You want to aim for slightly above what the buyers may expect. This will leave them feeling highly impressed with the house, and it will leave them feeling like the asking price is a really good deal for the house.

Look at Comparables

There are two ways you can investigate comparables in your area. First, you can go online and look at interior photos. While this will provide you with a lot of information, you are only seeing what the realtor wanted you to see when taking the photos.

Another, arguably, more effective strategy, is to actually go see comparables in your area. Talk to your realtor about setting up a few showings. This will give you a chance to experience the house as a prospective buyer. As you tour the house, look at the furniture, the accessories, and the overall look and feel of the house. Mentally compare it to your house. Does it feel bigger or smaller? Can you envision your stuff in the house or are you overwhelmed by the current owners' things? What would you do different if you were trying to sell the house?

Answering these questions will help you to prepare the house you are trying to sell. You want prospective buyers to feel your house is clean, spacious, and organized. In addition to seeing what isn't working in comparables, take note of things that impressed you. Can you re-create that feeling or experience in the house you're selling?

Know What Home Buyers Really Look For

You need to understand there are two basic features that all home buyers are looking for; they want a house that is spacious and low-maintenance. While there are buyers out there looking to downsize, research shows that most people are looking to move somewhere they feel is more spacious. Secondly, people are looking for houses that they feel will be low-maintenance. This is one of those things people may not say they are looking for, but if asked, they certainly wouldn't say they were looking for a house that was high-maintenance.

FACT

Homes with an open floor plan are the national bestsellers within the housing market. An open floor plan makes the kitchen the focal point or the hub of the home. When entertaining, an open floor plan encourages more engagement between the host and guests.

Spacious Living

Open floor plans are great for this, but you can create the illusion of more space with any floor plan. Most homeowners are looking for spacious homes that are clean, easy to maintain, and give off a positive feeling. They also like lots of storage space and rooms that provide options. For example, a room that could be used as a bedroom or an office is going to be more appealing than a room that is clearly meant to be an office.

There are a variety of ways you can achieve these goals. For example, simply making sure a room is well-lit can make it appear larger and more spacious. Presenting the house perfectly cleaned and with minimal furniture and décor will give the impression that the house is easy to maintain. Showing cabinets, bookshelves, and closets with minimal items in and on them will make them appear larger, and will increase the illusion of storage space.

In reality, the house may have the exact same amount of storage as the house for sale down the street. However, if your house is staged to increase the perception of storage while the other house is not, potential buyers are going to feel more drawn to the house you are selling.

Even if the house you are flipping is pretty small, there are things you can do to make it appear larger and more spacious. You only need to create the appearance of spaciousness. One thing you can do is use minimal furniture when staging the house. You don't want to show an empty house because then people might look at the rooms and think they are too small to fit their furniture. By using a minimal amount of furniture, the rooms will look larger because they have furniture in them, but there is still plenty of space to move around the room.

The accessories you use and where you put them will also play an important role in making the house feel more spacious. You want to use only a handful of accessories to avoid making the rooms look cluttered. For example, in the dining room, you want to use a small table so there is plenty of room to walk completely around the table. However, if you set the table, it will make the table look really small and cluttered. Instead, you can simply put a vase of fresh flowers or a bowl of fresh fruit in the center of the table.

Low Maintenance Living

The easiest way to create the illusion that a house is low maintenance is by having it perfectly clean when showing it to prospective buyers. If a buyer sees dust lining the fan blades and window sills, he'll just be reminded of how much work and cleaning he has at his own house. This is a negative feeling. Although it is fairly common sense that all houses require cleaning, you want to avoid reminding people of this while they are looking at the house.

When painting the interior of the house, you can use paints that make the walls easier to wash. When showing the house to a family with kids or pets, you can emphasize this point as a low maintenance feature.

Preparing to Stage a Home

Once the house is renovated, you are ready to start with the actual staging and decorating. If you go into the staging fully prepared, you can get it done in a day and have the house ready to show. If you are unsure about staging decisions, have your realtor come look at the house when you are done to provide professional feedback.

Needed Supplies

The amount of furniture and accessories you will need for this will depend on the size of the house. You will also need a variety of different sized Command Strips, a level, and cleaning supplies. Dusting spray, window cleaner, paper towels, lemon fresh floor cleaner, a mop, bucket, and vacuum will be the most important cleaning supplies. At this point, the deep cleaning should be done, but you will need to keep up on the light cleaning for each showing and open house.

Start with Cleaning

You'll hear over and over again that you need to make sure every room is clean. Since you didn't actually live in the house, you won't have the normal dirt and clutter homeowners typically have to deal with when trying to sell their house. However, being a construction zone, you'll be dealing with a lot of dirt, dust, and leftover materials. When you are staging the house to show potential buyers, they need to be able to envision moving in that day. Obviously, they won't be moving in that day, but they have to be able to picture it in their minds. This will not happen if they are looking at trash on the floor and a coating of drywall dust throughout the house.

The kitchen and bathrooms are the most important areas to clean. If the house is basically ready and you are heading over for a showing, always check the bathrooms and kitchen to make sure there aren't any surprises. Grab a damp rag or paper towel, and quickly wipe down all the counters. Wipe out the sinks, and make sure the toilet is sparkling.

Getting Furniture and Accessories

Your furniture needs are going to be basic. While you want everything to look clean and in great condition, you do not have to spend a lot or go high end. You can buy all new pieces, use items you already have at your disposal, or a combination of both. When gauging how much furniture you'll need, figure a bed and dresser for each bedroom. You can also use a nightstand for larger bedrooms. You will need basic living room furniture:

a couch, armchair, coffee table, and end table. You will need a small dining room table with four chairs for the dining room. You will also need a variety of smaller pieces. For example, you may need a small table for the entranceway, a dinette table for an eat-in kitchen, or a desk for a home office.

You'll only want a few accessories for each room. Fresh flowers are always a great choice for decorating throughout the house. Bowls of fresh fruit are also great for the dining room or kitchen. Wall art, mirrors, and clocks should be simple and larger, so they don't look lost on a larger wall. All wall accessories should be hung with Command Strips, so you aren't putting new holes in the freshly painted walls.

ESSENTIAL

Using simple and larger accessories will help make the house appear low maintenance. It doesn't matter that the buyers will be bringing in their own accessories that may or may not be easy to clean.

Decorating the House

It is important to make the house appear current and trendy. To get a feel for what is trendy in home décor, take time to look at current home décor magazines. Also take into consideration the neighborhood appeal. While you don't want to stick too closely to a particular style, you do want to appeal to local potential buyers. On average, a home buyer is looking at houses twelve miles from where they are currently living, so they are already comfortable with the local décor and style.

When decorating the house, it is also important to keep the style consistent throughout the house. You don't want to create a Victorian feel in the living room and a French Country feel in the kitchen. It will be distracting to the prospective buyers. Additionally, creating too much of a theme in decorating can be distracting.

Choosing Colors

For room colors, you want to keep things subtle. For example, if you decide to paint a bedroom green, go with a pale or seafoam green as opposed to an emerald green. The more dramatic the colors are, the less likely you are to appeal to the majority of buyers. It is best to choose neutral colors like cream, tan, off-white, or a soft gold. These colors will coordinate with nearly any color or style of furniture.

Choosing Accessories

Choose accessories that are contemporary and tasteful. Avoid dramatic pieces. Avoid accessories that are spiritual or political in nature. Avoid scented candles and air fresheners. You should also avoid alcohol-related décor or even having alcohol or wine bottles as part of your décor. These types of décor items have the strong potential of offending a potential buyer.

Finally, less is more should always be the theme. Flat surfaces should be basically clear. Don't put a multipiece decorative canister set on the kitchen counter. It will make the available space on the counter look smaller. Instead, go with a single candle, a small pot with fresh flowers, or a decorative bowl or fruit basket.

The less is more theme goes the same for wall décor. If there is a big open wall that looks bare with nothing on it, choose a single large item like an oversized clock or mirror as opposed to a cluster of pictures or wall vases. The large item will increase the illusion of a larger room by decreasing the visual clutter.

Curb Appeal?

Curb appeal is the first impression people get when they drive up to the house, park, and walk up to the front door. Curb appeal encompasses the yard, the walkway, the front of the house, and the entranceway. It is what people see driving down the street. In order to get a feel for your house's curb appeal, you should go to the road or even across the street to get a good look at the front of the house. What stands out when you look at the house? What do you see that doesn't look great? How can you make it look better and more inviting? These are the questions you need to ask yourself while looking at the front of the house.

FACT

Curb appeal is so important to the staging of a house, there is an entire show on HGTV that deals solely with teaching people how to improve their curb appeal. The show has been airing for over a decade due to its popularity.

How Important Is Curb Appeal?

Curb appeal is arguably one of the most important things you can go for when staging a house. Most prospective buyers will have an opinion about a house before they even walk in the door, and it is based solely on the house's curb appeal. Potential buyers should be impressed as they approach the house. If a prospective buyer is unimpressed by the curb appeal, they will go into the house with higher expectations. They will be looking to see if the inside of the house is as unimpressive as the outside and that will make them more critical.

How to Increase Curb Appeal

First, make sure the front yard is mowed and edged along the sidewalks and driveway. Make sure the driveway, sidewalks, and walkways are cleared and clean. You can power wash the paved areas to give them a fresh look. One of the easiest ways to stage the front of the house is by adding decorative planters with freshly planted flowers on either side of the door or walkway leading up to the door. Make sure the entranceway is clean. Put down a new welcome mat outside the front door.

What Not to Do When Staging

When staging a house, you need to keep your two primary goals in focus: create a spacious and low maintenance vibe. Other than ignoring these goals, there are only two things you want to really avoid while staging a house to sell: adding too much personality and not doing enough cleaning before people tour the house.

Too Much Personality

Don't only choose accessories that you love. Your taste is not going to be shared by all people. Choose colors and accessories that are relatively neutral and trendy. Also, do not create themes in rooms. People often want to create nautical or beach themes in bathrooms. Don't do that. It will turn away prospective buyers that aren't interested in that type of theme. Even if the theme can be easily changed by taking out the accessories, most people can't visualize rooms being different than the way they've previously seen it. If a house has a nautical-themed bathroom, this is what they will remember about the house.

Not Enough Cleaning

Cleaning has been talked about a few times in this chapter because cleaning is so important. Few things will turn away potential buyers faster than touring a dirty house. Even if the house is just dusty, it subconsciously sends a negative message to the brain of your prospective buyer.

CHAPTER 15

Staging Room by Room

When staging the house, you will move from room to room to ensure that each room is clean, decorated, and arranged the way you want it to be. There are ideas and strategies for each room that will help you enhance the appeal of that particular room. While individual room ideas will vary, the underlying goals will be the same. You want the rooms to feel and appear spacious and well-maintained. Well-maintained means clean and in good repair. Every room without exception has to be clean. When cleaning, be sure to clean the room from top to bottom. Start with the ceiling, the tops of the windows, lighting, and fan blades to make sure there is no residual dust or debris from the renovations. Make sure none of the walls are scuffed, and the floor is clean. If it is a hard floor, polish it prior to moving in the furniture. You want to keep in mind the kind of buyer you want to attract and then make all your staging decisions based on this buyer.

Exterior

Staging the exterior of a home is about creating curb appeal that sets the stage for the rest of the home tour. Exterior staging is also important as it sends a message about the condition and maintenance of the home. Curb appeal is the appearance of the house from the street and how it appears as you approach the entrance. The curb appeal focuses on the features of the home and yard that face the street. This is important to remember if your home is on a corner lot; don't ignore the side yard. Exterior staging includes the front and backyards, driveway, walkways, lighting, and entrance. Finally, in addition to being clean and inviting, you want the exterior of the home to be on par with the asking price.

Front and Backyards

The front and back yards should be freshly mowed, weeds pulled, shrubs and plants nicely trimmed, and hopefully, flowers blooming. If the weather is nice, you can always plant flowers as part of your staging. If the weather makes it impractical to plant flowers, you can always place potted flowers near the front entrance. Finally, ensure there is adequate lighting and that all lights work.

ESSENTIAL

Even though the backyard isn't part of the "curb appeal," it is important to make sure it is cleaned, maintained, and ready to show. Prospective buyers will make their way through the house and look at the backyard.

Hardscapes

Hardscapes include the driveway, sidewalks, pathways, and decking. Use a power washer to clean all surfaces. Fill and repair cracks in concrete surfaces where feasible. In the case of blacktop surfaces, repairing and resealing will give them a fresh new look. Remove weeds that grow up between hardscape joints.

Exterior Home Appearance

Start with power washing the exterior surface of the home as well as any outbuildings. Paint exterior surfaces that need painting. Peeling and chipped paint is an indication of deferred maintenance and causes a potential buyer to question what other maintenance issues may exist. This gives the potential buyer ammunition to present a lower offer. Just as painting a home can support an asking price, washing and repairing all windows and screens is a necessity. Plus, clean windows mean more sunlight shining into your home and a well-lit interior creates a clean and welcoming space.

Entryway

The front entrance is an important one. It begins when your buyers step on the porch or front step and doesn't end until they have left your foyer. The entrance should be clean and inviting, but not cluttered.

Exterior

You want to make sure the house numbers are clear and visible from the road. The front door should be clean and freshly painted. If you have a porch, consider one or two chairs, appropriately sized for the space, and a small table. Another alternative is a hanging bench with a couple of brightly colored pillows. Finally, a few carefully selected potted plants are a great option to liven up the space. If you don't have a porch, a single potted plant and a welcome mat are sufficient.

Foyer

The foyer is very important because it is the first peek of the interior that prospective buyers will get to see. It is also the first room guests will see as they enter the house, so prospective buyers will have that in mind as they enter. You want this room to appear welcoming and organized, and to act as a sneak peek to the quality and cleanliness of the rest of the house. The foyer is either part of a hallway, a small room, or virtually nonexistent if the front door opens up right into the living room. When the entranceway is simply part of a larger room, you want the space to flow with the rest of the room. However, you also want people to feel there is somewhere to take off their shoes and hang their coat.

Keep decorating to a minimum. Consider a small table, if space permits, and wall décor. A small decorative mirror is often helpful because it will visually enlarge the area, but makes even a small space more functional and attractive. If there is no coat closet, a coat rack or wall hooks will do. These are particularly important when you are showing the house during colder months. If people are wearing coats or jackets, they will immediately become aware of the fact there is nowhere for guests to put their coats by the door.

Generally speaking, potential buyers will buy the illusion of organization. If you place a decorative bowl on a table, toss a set of keys in there. Also, consider adding a decorative basket with a few pieces of mail in it. This will give the illusion of organization. However, it is important to add only one set of keys or literally two pieces of mail. Filling the bowl with keys or the basket with too much mail will make things look cluttered.

Public Spaces

Public spaces include the living room, dining room, kitchen, media room, and main floor powder room. Think of these rooms as places where you would entertain guests that are not spending the night. These rooms should feel bright, spacious, and welcoming. Your prospective buyer should be able to see herself and her friends spending time together in these spaces.

Living/Family Room

Furniture needs to be scaled to the room and include all the basic elements: seating, table, and lighting. When it comes to the living room or main area, size and organization are what you need to be selling. You should stage the room with minimal furniture. A couch and either a love seat, or a few chairs are most ideal. Add a coffee table and two side tables. The coffee table should be clean and clear. You can add a coffee table picture book or a small tray with a candle garden as decoration, but the majority of the table should be cleared off. You really shouldn't have any more furniture than that, and if it is a particularly small living room, you should go with even less.

Avoid having furniture pushed to the perimeter of a room and pushed against the wall. If using an area rug, ensure the rug is appropriately sized to the room as it anchors the space. Consider a rug that allows all pieces of furniture in the space to have the front legs on the rug and the back legs off. Use furniture pieces that are neutral in color, and accessories (pillows, throws, vases, art, etc.) to add pops of color. If the room has a fireplace with a mantel, the mantel should also have minimal coordinating decorations. The area directly around the opening of the fireplace should be completely clear.

Avoid having any room décor items on the floor, such as plants, statues, or baskets. The more floor space that is visible, the larger the room will look. Depending on the size and layout of the living room, an area slightly larger than the length of the couch can also add to the special feel of the space.

QUESTION

What should you do if the living room is just really small?
One thing you can do is stage the room with a smaller couch (not a love seat, just a smaller couch). It will give the illusion of more space because they'll be looking at what appears to be a regular-sized couch with plenty of space to move around the room.

For wall décor, add a mirror or large-framed painting to the largest wall in the room. If you go with a painting, make it a calming, scenic painting with warm colors. This will help increase the good feeling generated from seeing the room. Windows should be lightly dressed, meaning they should look finished, but not frilly. But, if hanging drapes, ensure they are fully open. This will maximize the amount of natural light coming into the room.

You also want to have three lamps in the room: two table lamps for the side tables and one floor lamp. This way, if the house is being shown on a day or at a time without a lot of natural light, there can still be a great deal of light in the room. Having lots of light will make the rooms look larger and more spacious. It will also make it easier for potential buyers to see the cleanliness of the room.

Dining Room

If there is a formal dining room, you want it to be clear. Don't put items in the dining room that make it appear to be a multiuse room like a desk or a microwave stand. You want prospective buyers to visualize family dinners, entertaining, and peaceful evenings when they enter the dining room.

For the dining room, it is important that potential buyers can completely walk around the table without feeling crowded. For that reason, you should keep the furniture to one four-person table with four chairs. If it is a really big dining room, you can add a buffet, but only if you can still comfortably walk between the table and the buffet without feeling crowded.

On the table, you can add a simple table runner or placemats at each chair setting. A lot of people set the table like they're about to sit down to dinner. Don't do that unless you're planning to go in each day and wipe everything down. If the plates or silverware get dusty, it will have a very negative affect on potential buyers.

ESSENTIAL

Having the table fully set will make the table look crowded. It is also unnatural. It would not feel normal to walk in and see the table set like people are about to have dinner.

Add an area rug slightly larger than the table as well. Generally, people prefer hardwood floors in dining rooms because it is easier to clean spills and food crumbs. However, it's also more comfortable to rest your feet on carpeting while dining as opposed to a hard and potentially cold floor. An area rug provides the best of both worlds.

Kitchen

The kitchen is one of the most important rooms in the house. For many people, the kitchen is the central hub of their home. The kitchen needs to appear spacious, impeccably clean, and organized. An open floor plan is best, but if the house doesn't have one, you need to make the kitchen feel as spacious as possible.

Cleaning is the number one thing you can do to stage a kitchen. There is no such thing as a "too clean" kitchen. You even want it to smell clean. Use citrus cleaning when washing the floors and counters. Run citrus peels (e.g., oranges, lines, or lemons) through the garbage disposal before a showing to eliminate any offending smells coming from the drains. A citrus smell makes people think clean; that is why so many kitchen cleaners are citrus smelling.

The kitchen is one of the most important rooms in the house, and likewise, it is one of the most important rooms to stage. The kitchen needs to be bathed in light. Keep the windows wide open and make sure there is ample overhead light. If there are extra lights over the sink or stove, have them on also. The massive amount of light will emphasize the cleanliness of the kitchen.

Private Spaces

Private spaces include the bedrooms, bathrooms, and home office. Think of these rooms as places that are reserved for you, your family, and the occasional overnight guest. Like public spaces, these rooms should feel bright, spacious, and welcoming, but they should also seem warm and relaxing.

Bedrooms

As with all rooms, the furniture in a bedroom needs to be scaled to the room and include all basic elements: bed, bedside table, dresser, and lighting. Beds should be made and the room should smell fresh. If it is a particularly large bedroom, you can add a vanity or dressing table. Another possible add-on for a large bedroom is an end of the bed bench with storage. In terms of cleaning, the biggest issue for bedrooms is the carpets. Avoid using overly fragranced carpet powders; they tend to be overwhelming. You want the room to smell fresh as opposed to scented. Finally, it is important to remember that you are trying to sell the perfect life. You want potential buyers to feel like their perfect life is possible in this house. This goes along with selling the illusion of organization.

ALERT

If the house is on the market for a couple weeks, you may need to go through and dust all the hard surfaces and wash the comforters on the beds. You don't want prospective buyers to come in and see a comforter covered in dust.

The bed should be the main focus of the room. While the master bedroom should have a full or queen, the other bedrooms should have twin beds. This will make it obvious to potential buyers which bedroom is the master bedroom. But, you don't need to buy a bed. Create the illusion of a bed. Inflate a small air mattress and put it on top of milk crates. Then make the bed like normal. As long as no one sits on the bed, they won't realize it isn't a real bed. All surfaces should be free of clutter, but not barren. A book or candle on the bedside table creates an illusion of a lifestyle that you want your buyers to see and feel.

If the house has a master bedroom, you want to make that room appear larger and more impressive than the other bedrooms. Master bedrooms are generally the largest of the bedrooms with the largest closets or even multiple closets. In the master bedroom, you want the dressers, bedside tables, and bedside lamps to match. You want the bedspread and décor to be in warm soothing colors.

The other bedrooms should be devoid of age-specific decorations. This will leave them open to being rooms for little kids, older kids, or other adults that will be living there. Similarly, you want to avoid making one room look like a girl's room, while another room looks like a boy's room. This can be distracting and cause you to lose potential buyers that don't have children that fit in the demographics you made the rooms for.

However, if your likely prospective buyers are families, then staging one of the bedrooms as a child's room or nursery is acceptable. In a child's room, it is okay to use colors other than strictly neutral ones, but keep the colors soft, pleasant, and muted: green, blue, lavender, or yellow are all okay.

Decorate a well-made bed with a single doll or stuffed animal. A desk in the room can be staged with things like a coloring book and crayons, a desk lamp, reading books, or other similar accessories.

Bathrooms

The bathrooms are as important as the kitchen in terms of cleanliness and staging. Avoid decorating with themes. Avoid overly floral décor or childish décor. The bathrooms should be neutral in color and without a gender preference. It is important to do what you can to make the bathroom feel as spacious as possible. While this may be difficult for really small bathrooms, you need to do what you can. Low cost updates to a bathroom include paint, lighting, and sink faucets. Other updates for a larger budget include new flooring, new bath/shower fixtures, and an updated toilet.

Remove any extra furniture or cabinets from the bathroom. Although this may take away from the storage, it will make the bathroom appear more spacious. Also, for really small bathrooms, it is better to install a pedestal sink instead of a vanity. This will increase the floor space, which will make the room look larger. Remove carpet and toilet rug sets. Add a new shower curtain and curtain liner. If the shower has doors, make sure they are perfectly clean. The door tracks will need to be cleaned as well. Make sure the bathroom is very bright. Increased lighting always helps a room appear larger. However, it will also highlight dirt faster, so cleaning is, once again, essential.

FACT

Having a room that can serve as a home office is a great selling point. It makes people feel they will have extra space for the things they want whether that is a home office, a craft room, or a media room.

Home Office

Creating a home office is an ideal staging for a room that wouldn't work well as a bedroom or if there are already several bedrooms in the house. Even people who don't work from home like having a home office. Once again, it sells the illusion of organization and the perfect life. With a home office, there is no need to sit at the dining room table to pay bills or let mail stack up on the kitchen counter.

You can place a desk, file cabinet, and bookshelf in the home office. If it's a larger room, you can also stage an armchair near the bookshelf to add the idea of having a quiet area to read. For the bookshelf, add some books to each shelf. Alternate the side of the shelf the books sit on so it looks organized as opposed to leaving the shelves bare. For the desk, add a desk lamp and some basic accessories; these can include a pencil holder or a desk blotter. Depending on the size of the room, you should also add a floor lamp next to the armchair. This will help you to maximize the amount of light in the room.

Utility Spaces

Utility spaces include laundry rooms, mud rooms, and closets. These spaces address the functionality of a home and are an important, but often overlooked, space. Again, like any space in the home, these rooms need to be clean and organized.

Laundry Room

You may or may not be selling your house with the washer and dryer included, but this is something to consider. The first-time homebuyer may not have a washer and dryer yet. Finding the washer and dryer in your house could be just the incentive your prospective buyer needs. Laundry space should be clean and well-lit. While not ordinarily recommended in other rooms, white is a great color for a laundry room. This is especially true if the laundry is located in a basement where the amount of natural light is reduced. If the laundry room is large enough, consider installing a work surface for sorting and folding laundry.

Mud Room

Contrary to its name, this room should be anything but muddy. Again, clean and well-lit is the rule. You'll want this room to appear as spacious as possible. Avoid having things set on the floor; wall-mounted hooks, a bench to sit down on, and room for your boots is perfect.

Closets

All the closets throughout the house can be treated the same. The goal is to show off how much storage the house has, as well as how easy it is to keep the house organized and clean. If there is carpeting inside the closets, make sure it is vacuumed. Make sure that if there is a closet rod or shelves inside the closet, they are level and sturdy.

ESSENTIAL

Make sure the closet shelves are dusted. Add a mild smelling sachet or air freshener in each closet to keep them from smelling stale.

All closets and storage areas should be giving the illusion of space and organization. With that in mind, you don't want them to be completely empty. This will make them look stark, and most buyers will only imagine their own disorganized closets, as opposed to visualizing the potential of organization. Instead, you want to have some stuff in the closets, but not a lot. This will make the closets look large and easy to organize. The same goes for coat closets, linen closets, pantry closets, and all other storage areas. For example, the linen closet should have one or two sheet sets, and two or three towels.

Unfinished Spaces

Unfinished spaces include the basement, garage, attic, and any other out-buildings or other unfinished storage spaces. For most prospective buyers, these unfinished spaces are a bonus because they mean more room for their stuff. But, these spaces can also be intimidating and downright scary if they are dark, dank, and dungeon-like. As a side note, if these spaces have not been finished, you would stage them as though they have been finished (e.g., bedroom, den, office, etc.).

Basement and Attics

Unfinished basements and attics should be staged as clean and usable storage areas. You want to emphasize the fact that they are clean and dry.

The best thing you can do for staging is make sure the areas are extremely well lit. This is especially true for basements; you don't want potential buyers to get the "dark damp" basement feel when they go in the basement. Make sure the area is completely clean and well-lit. You can do this by making sure all the overhead lights have light bulbs with the maximum possible wattage. Daylight bulbs are also a great option as the light they emit is a whiter, brighter light. The same goes for attics. Maximize the light in the attic as much as you can.

Garages and Outbuildings

For the garage, you want to stage it to show as a space that can be used for both vehicles and storage. Make sure the garage doors are in good shape and that the automated door opener works. Garages and outbuildings should be staged with functionality in mind. This means they should be well-lit and clean. Consider installing pegboard on a wall and if the size of space will accommodate a workbench or table, this is another good option.

Outdoor Entertainment Spaces

Outdoor entertainment spaces include decks, patio, pools, fire pits, and water features. Depending on the house and the neighborhood it's located in, these features may not even be an issue. However, if your home has any of these features, then they need to be staged as well.

Decks and Patios

Like the hardscapes referenced earlier in this chapter, decks and patios need to be clean and in good repair. Depending on the size, these spaces can be staged with a café table, a couple of chairs, or even a few deck chairs. Large spaces may be able to accommodate an outdoor sectional sofa. Be sure that the style and color pallet of your outdoor spaces are consistent with the style and color pallet of your indoor spaces. Use neutral colors with throw pillows to add pops of color. Add colorful lanterns and a plastic water pitcher and glasses to a table top. Like your outdoor spaces, make sure you have plenty of functional lighting.

Anytime you have a storm coming through, it is a good idea to go check on the patio, deck, and pool to make sure there isn't any debris, and all your lounge chairs are safe and upright.

Pools

Pools present their own issues. If your home has a pool, it needs to be clean, functional, and safe. Pool mechanical systems should be in good working order and outer housings clean and intact. Consider having the pool inspected in advance of any showing; this will ensure the systems are working properly and build credibility with prospective buyers. The pool should have a gate and cover, should be functional, and in good shape. Lastly, stage the area with a couple of lounge chairs and small table. Your buyers should see themselves relaxing by the pool.

Fire Pits and Water Features

As with all things discussed, fire pits and water features should be clean. Gas lines, electric starters, and pumps should all be functioning. These features are often located on or near a deck, patio, or pool. If this is the case, they should enhance the space rather than distract or detract from it. If your water feature includes fish, make sure all the fish are alive. This should be checked regularly; should the unfortunate happen, you don't want your prospective buyer finding the fish. If the pond doesn't hold fish, consider installation of some water lilies.

In cases where the fire pit or water feature is a stand-alone feature, they should be highlighted accordingly. Options include having a walkway leading to them or a seating arrangement nearby where they can be enjoyed. For more rustic fire pits, consider having a stack of fresh cut wood with a couple of logs in the fire pit. Another way to highlight these features is with ornamental lighting such as decorative, solar powered, ground lights, or underwater lighting.

CHAPTER 16

Marketing Your House to Sell

Marketing your house to sell is an invaluable process. You already know the faster you are able to sell the property, the faster you will recoup your investment and make a profit. The housing market can be a competitive one, which is why it is essential to effectively market your house across multiple channels simultaneously. Marketing includes both online and offline activities. You don't need to be a marketing professional to effectively market your house, but you do need to understand what works and what doesn't.

Strategies That Work

When considering your different options in marketing, you want to focus on the strategies that are effective while also being cost efficient. When deciding how to market the house, talk to your realtor first, if you are working with one. Your realtor should certainly be able to help tremendously with this part, as it is also in his best interest to sell the house quickly. There are three options in offline marketing that you should consider: print advertising, yard signs, and networking.

Print Advertising

This includes advertising in local papers and house sale magazines. This type of advertising can be costly depending on the area you are living in. However, if you are planning a large open house, you may want to take the chance. A lot of people still check the newspaper when looking for local open houses. Print advertising is also a great way to get your name out there. This is helpful if you really build your flipping business and have houses to sell on a regular basis.

ESSENTIAL

Check the difference in price between a printed classified ad and an ad with a picture included. Publishing ads with pictures is more effective because it catches the reader's attention and stands out among all the other ads. However, it can also be very expensive.

Yard Signs

Yard signs have proven to be very effective. For many people thinking about buying a house, it is not uncommon to drive around the neighborhoods where they want to live in search of "For Sale" signs. Sometimes people aren't necessarily looking to buy a house, but simply driving through a neighborhood they really like and see a "For Sale" sign. Yard signs also encourage word-of-mouth marketing. Neighbors are more likely to tell people they know are looking to buy a house. Yard signs can be purchased for a relatively inexpensive price at a hardware store or through a printing company. You can even order generic "For Sale" signs featuring your company name and contact information, so the same sign can be used over and over again. If you are working with a realtor, they likely already have signs that can be used at your property, so this will be a nonexpense.

Networking

Another important form of marketing that people often overlook is networking. Let people know you have a house for sale. Offer a referral fee to anyone who finds you a legitimate buyer. See if there are any professional organizations in your area that cater to landlords or other property investors. For example, in Lorain County, Ohio, there is an organization called the Lake Erie Landlord Association. They have monthly meetings and part of their monthly meeting is what they call "Buy, Sell, and Trade." This is a time when members can stand up and make announcements regarding properties they have for sale. Other members may be interested in buying the house or they can help spread the word. These types of organizations can be crucial to your long-term success as a house flipper.

Accurately Pricing the House

While this may not be an obvious marketing strategy, it is probably one of the most important. Accurate pricing is essential in order to get people to actually visit the house for a showing. Houses that are priced too high will sit on the market because there are too many other options selling for better prices. Houses that are priced too low might sell quickly, but you'll be losing money on the opportunity. Plus, you might have people who don't look because they assume with such a low asking price, there must be something wrong with the house.

Strategies to Avoid

Just as there are successful strategies that you should focus on when marketing your house, there are strategies that you should avoid. These strategies aren't necessarily ineffective, but their level of effectiveness is not enough to justify the time, energy, and money that goes into them.

Television Realty Shows

Some realty companies still air television shows where they showcase the houses they have for sale. While seeing your house on television might be fun, it is hardly an effective strategy. The market for those shows is very narrow and depending on how you get showcased, it can be expensive. When compared to online advertising outlets, the television shows are archaic.

Flier Boxes

You can get a clear plastic box to put outside the house for fliers. These are ineffective for several reasons. First, the fliers tend to be taken by anyone walking down the street. People grab them out of curiosity and then don't put them back. Also, fliers get ruined after the first rain because the boxes are not water sealed. As long as your yard sign has the needed contact information on it, there is no reason an interested buyer would need a flier on the spot. If someone walking by is really interested, they can look the house up online or call the number provided to get more information.

ALERT

There is some debate over the effectiveness of flier boxes. If you are working with a realtor that swears by them and they are covering the cost of the fliers, it's worth trying. Even if it doesn't help, it won't cost you anything.

Creating Your Own Website

Even though you're starting out with just one property, you want to be prepared for your business to grow quickly. Starting a website now will enable you to start building your online presence, so that when you have houses for sale, you are already established online. Additionally, you can advertise other companies through your website and make your website independently profitable as part of your overall business.

Setting Up a Website

The first step to creating your own website is choosing a domain name that will accurately represent your company and is available through domain registries. Once you find a domain name, you will need to buy it to ensure no one else will.

The second step is to set your website up with a content management system (CMS). Popular CMSs include WordPress and Joomla. These offer drag and drop features, which allow you to design your own website without really knowing HTML. While there may still be situations where you will need specialized design with HTML, you can hire someone to handle that for you.

Once your website is published, you'll need to start adding content. This is also something you can hire out relatively inexpensively. Until you start having houses ready to sell, you can build your website by adding content to a blog on your website. Your blog can cover topics related to real estate, selling houses, staging houses, and flipping houses. This will help you grow a reader base.

Advertising Houses Through Your Website

When you do have a house ready to sell, you can post all your house's information on your website. As you post ads on other websites, you can include links back to your website. You can also set up an interactive calendar, which would allow people to schedule a showing right from your website, or if you are working with a realtor, you can have a link to your realtor's contact information.

It is important to keep your website regularly updated. New content should be added at least a couple times a week. Search engines monitor web activity when choosing relevant websites for search results.

QUESTION

Is Internet marketing really that important?
These days, Internet marketing is essential. You can't just stick a sign out front and hope for the best. You need to be highly proactive, and Internet marketing is the most effective way to do that.

Internet Marketing

Internet marketing has become a significant source of marketing for real estate. Many buyers, particularly young buyers, are looking online before contacting realtors or sellers. They want to gather as much information as they can to make an informed decision more quickly. For that reason, it is essential that you have an online marketing strategy, and you make sure all the vital information regarding the properties you have for sale is easily accessible online.

Content Marketing

Content marketing refers to the marketing of content you create and post online. This can include written content, images, and videos. Content marketing, if done correctly, can be highly effective. The one downside to marketing a house online yourself is that the big realty companies already have a significant amount of clout online in regard to search engine rankings, so you will need to work harder to be seen.

The first thing you want to do is write a detailed description of the property. Write a description of each room and significant feature in the house. You want to use a lot of descriptive words to make the house sound as amazingly inviting and desirable as possible. You then need to take your written description, the images you took and edited for marketing purposes, and the video you created, and post them online in as many different places as you can.

Writing Sales Copy

Writing sales copy is an industry of its own. It is a way of writing that makes the product appeal to consumers on a psychological level. Copywriters are well trained in how to use descriptive words and phrases to get an emotional reaction out of readers. While you can't learn how to be an effective copywriter overnight, you can pursue ways to improve the quality of your descriptions. To do this, you can hire a copywriter to write your descriptions for you. You can learn basic copywriting and do it yourself, or you can hire a copywriter, who is willing to work with you to help you improve your own descriptions. The path you choose will depend on how much time and money you want to invest in getting this done. This is one example of when it might be best to preserve your time for more important tasks and hiring someone to write the descriptions for you.

Social Media Marketing

Social media marketing is another effective branch of online marketing. To market your house through social media, you need to strategically post the descriptions, images, and video you created to multiple social networks and web pages. For example, search Facebook for any local pages that allow people to post things they have for sale. You should do the same with Twitter and Google+. Post images of the house on Instagram and Pinterest. Post the video of your house on YouTube.

ALERT

Once a house sells, you want to take down your online ads. Taking down your video tour on YouTube is also a good idea. Otherwise, people may get frustrated if they check several ads only to discover the house has already been sold.

With every social network posting, you should include links back to your website or the base website where your sales information is posted. In addition to including links back to your website, you should include contact information with every posting. You can't assume people will follow your links.

Encourage your friends and family to like and share your posts. Although they may not be personally interested, every time they like or share the post, all of their social contacts will see the post. The more the information is shared, the better your chances will be to reach the people actually looking to buy.

Virtual Staging

Another thing you can do is offer virtual staging. There are a couple of ways you can go about this. First, you can stage the house prior to taking pictures, so when people look online, it will be exactly what they see if they visit the house. Another thing you can do is create an interactive floor plan. This will allow users to see how furniture can be arranged in the space. If they have the measurements for their furniture, they can make sure it will fit in various rooms, as well as through the doorway or up the stairs. Virtual staging can increase the likelihood that searchers will visit the actual house.

Creating Marketing Material

If you are not working with a realtor, you will need to create your own marketing material. Even if you are working with a realtor, you may want to be involved in the creation of marketing material to ensure it is done to your standards. It requires only a brief search online to find humorous marketing failures committed by realtors. Additionally, understanding the type of marketing materials you need and the standard you want them to be at will help you to know quickly if the realtor is not doing a great job.

Fliers

Fliers are ideal for marketing because they can be posted in places where potential buyers may see them, they can be included in information boxes, and they can be passed out at showings, so potential buyers remember which houses they saw and liked. Fliers should include photos of the house and essential information like the address, asking price, number of bedrooms and bathrooms, and any other information that may give the house an advantage over other houses in the area.

Photos

You need high-quality photos of the interior and exterior of the house to include with all marketing material. The photos should not be taken until the house is renovated, cleaned, and ready to sell. Take a minute to search online for bad realtor photos, you will find dozens of examples of what not to do: bad pictures, bad angles, fuzzy images, etc. These images need to visually sell the house. If prospective buyers aren't impressed by the images, they aren't going to waste their time going to see the house in person.

Video

Do a walk-through of the house with your camera and create a video tour. People who are researching houses online like to get as much information as they can before actually making an appointment to see a house. A video tour will help them decide if they are interested, which will save you the time and energy of working with people who aren't really potential buyers.

Video tours will be highly informative and helpful for prospective buyers, but they will also help you attract more attention through search engines when people are searching for houses in your area.

When creating the video, be sure to show the entire house. Walk slowly and be careful not to rock or shake the camera too much; you don't want to make viewers sick. Speak slowly and clearly while narrating the tour. You can choose to have voice-over narration, or you can have someone in the video actually talking and pointing out different features while you film.

Finally, have the video edited. Simply taking a video yourself and then posting it online will make it look and feel like a home video. You want this to be professional looking. It isn't just selling your house; it is helping you to create your brand. If you do not know how to edit the video yourself, you can hire a freelancer to do it for you. It will be worth the money to have a professional-looking virtual tour video.

Selling Binders

A selling binder is essentially an overview of the property for the new homeowners. It includes proof of major items that have been recently replaced such as the roof, windows, furnace, or hot water heater. These are expensive and major repairs, so showing potential homeowners that these repairs have already been made adds value to the house.

The selling binder should also include any warranties that come with the repairs that have been made. The new owners will need all this information if they need work done in the near future. The selling binder should also include pictures of the house and the interior rooms. It should highlight the aspects of the house that increase its value compared to houses in the area.

You want to have the selling binder available for people to look through during open houses and showings. A great way to do this is to simply leave it out on the kitchen counter and let people know they are welcome to take a look. You should also bring the selling binder with you when you attend networking events. This way, if someone shows interest in the house, you can let them look through the selling binder.

Business Cards

You will need to create business cards with all of your contact information including your website, cell-phone number, and e-mail address. Whenever you are networking with other property investors, you can give them a card. When you hear someone talking about buying a house, you can give him a card. You can have friends and family pass your cards along to people they know are interested in buying a house. Let everyone know they should watch your website to see the houses you have available.

Open Houses and Showings

Open houses and showings are opportunities for potential buyers to tour the house, ask questions, and decide if they are interested. The open house is like the big production you've been carefully planning for. You want the house to look its best, and you want the open house to be well-advertised so a lot of people show up. Having a large number of people come to the open house will increase your networking opportunities and word-of-mouth advertising, and it will promote the house in the minds of those that attend. They will see how many other people appear to be interested in the house, and that will increase the pressure to make an offer quickly.

ESSENTIAL

Don't feel like you have to go over the top during an open house. While a cheese tray and bottled water is nice to be able to offer people, you don't need to have a buffet of snacks available.

226

Preparing for an Open House or Showing

Before each open house or showing, you should go through the house quickly and look for any messes that may have been missed or left behind by mistake. Have a trash bag, a roll of paper towels, and a bottle of all purpose cleaner with you, just in case. Even if it is something as little as a dusty sink, you can quickly clean it up.

You also want to make sure there are high wattage light bulbs in every light fixture and that all the lights are turned on when the prospective buyers get there. Lighting up a room can make it look larger, cleaner, and more inviting. Finally, you want to make sure all the windows are clean and clear. Clean windows will allow more natural light into the house, but they also make the house appear more appealing. Dirty windows are easy to notice.

Post-Open House Evaluation

After each open house, it is good to take some time to consider some of the feedback you received from the visitors. Was there something a majority of the people complained about? If so, is it something you could quickly and easily fix? Is there something a majority of the people liked that you could promote at your next open house or showing?

Developing a Practical Strategy

With so many marketing strategies at your disposal, it is best to create a practical marketing strategy that you will follow utilizing both online and offline marketing tactics. Creating an actual plan will ensure that everything is done effectively and appropriately. Going into a marketing campaign without a plan will result in things being missed, as well as overall stress and frustration. The easiest way to make sure everything is completed and without stress is to plan everything out in advance. This is not a situation where "winging it" will be effective. It is important to remember that every day you are in possession of the house, it is costing you money. The goal is to sell it and sell it fast.

Creating a Marketing Calendar

A significant part of your marketing strategy will be creating a marketing calendar. This will include the dates that ads will be in the newspaper and published online. It will also include the deadlines for newspaper and other outlets to ensure the information is published on the days you want it to be public. Your calendar should include when and where you will be getting the fliers printed and yard signs prepared. Every marketing activity you partake in should be scheduled, so you don't miss deadlines.

ESSENTIAL

Your marketing calendar for each house can be part of your greater editorial calendar, which will include when you will add new posts to your blog and what topics they will cover. It is best to use one calendar for all your business needs to avoid things being overlooked.

Delegating Marketing Tasks

If you are working with a realtor, she will be able to handle a great deal of the marketing tasks; that is her job. Additionally, the fliers and signs can come from the realtor, so these are two less tasks you will need to worry about. Let your realtor know what tasks you will accomplish and when you will accomplish them. For example, your realtor will be able to get your house listed on realty websites and added to the MLS. While she is handling that, you may be able to help by listing the property, videos, and images on your blog or website, your social networks, and other online resources you can work with.

If you aren't working with a realtor, you will need to assume the tasks a realtor would normally accomplish. There is a lot to be done, so if you have a business partner or assistant, it is a good idea to divide up the tasks. You focus on the tasks you are best at, and delegate the tasks that someone else can accomplish faster and more effectively. If you are delegating work to an assistant, you can also include busy work on his to-do list. For example, if you create the marketing fliers, your assistant can make sure they get printed. If you create the newspaper ad, your assistant can get it to the newspaper before the publishing deadline. When delegating tasks, do so in an effective manner. Don't just randomly split the to-do list in half and start working.

CHAPTER 17

Managing Multiple Flips

You may have a little overlap between two flips, or you may be running five flips at a time. Either way, you will need to develop effective strategies to keep everything organized and to stay on top of each project. Even with five projects going, you will only make money when the houses sell, so you need to be focused on finishing and selling the houses as quickly as possible.

Considering Locations

When you are managing multiple flips, you will need to frequently travel between the properties, as well as between the properties, your home, and supply stores. There are two basic strategies you can choose to adopt. You can intentionally look for houses in close proximity to each other, or you can just look for houses that meet your criteria regardless of their location. While neither strategy is particularly wrong, it is important to always keep your options open, so even if you choose to find houses close to each other, don't turn away from an ideal property that might be in the next town.

Advantages of Grouping Properties Together

The greatest advantage to grouping properties together is their proximity to each other. You'll easily be able to travel back and forth between the houses to keep tabs on the progress. If there is a problem at one house, you can quickly get there from the other house. You can also save time and, possibly, money with deliveries. Letting the delivery company know the houses are really close to each other can be the basis for negotiations regarding delivery costs or time of delivery.

If you are using the same contractors at multiple properties, it will also be easier for the contractors to stay in contact with both projects, and to move workers between the projects, as needed. There are clearly advantages to keeping the properties close to each other.

Disadvantages of Grouping Properties Together

There are two primary disadvantages to following this strategy. The first disadvantage is that you will be eliminating a lot of potentially great properties. As mentioned earlier, you want to try to keep your options open in regard to where you look for houses. Your underlying goal is to maximize and protect your profits, which means, in part, finding houses that are a great deal and require minimal renovations. You might not find multiple properties within close proximity of each other.

Secondly, if the renovations are done within a small timeframe, you will have multiple properties on the market simultaneously. This can create unneeded competition between the houses for potential buyers. One way to mitigate this disadvantage is to stagger your house purchases so the renovations are completed at different times. You can also work this into an advantage by allowing prospective buyers to see multiple homes you are selling; you may be more likely to sell one of them.

Negotiating Several Contracts

For each house you flip, you will be negotiating your buying and selling contracts. If you are in the process of flipping multiple houses, this can create a lot of paperwork, as well as a lot of mental work. It is essential that you keep your projects organized. Mixing up notes on different houses can lead to serious errors in your negotiations. In addition to staying organized and keeping your paperwork organized, working with a realtor will help tremendously. It will also help to have an office manager or assistant. Although you can start house flipping on your own, managing multiple flips is a tremendous job, and not one you will likely be able to handle on your own. Before jumping into multiple properties, you may want to think about your options. Even if you don't have an office to work from, you can hire a virtual assistant to keep up with the paperwork and documentation for you.

Making Bulk Deals

If you are willing and able to purchase multiple properties simultaneously, you can look into buying multiple properties owned by the same bank or seller. This will give you a negotiating point. You can make an offer on multiple properties together as part of one deal. The offer you prepare can include a "bulk rate" discount for buying them all at once. Although this might sound a bit unorthodox, it is not uncommon.

Organizing Paperwork

Even if you negotiate a bulk deal on multiple properties, each property will have its own deed and its own sales paperwork. It is important to organize them separately so that all the receipts and expenses get attributed to the correct property. This is necessary when determining the profit for each property, but also for when you file your taxes.

Organizing Multiple Timelines

For each property you are flipping, you will have a renovation timeline to follow. Depending on how far apart each house was started and what renovations are needed, you will be overseeing multiple crews and projects simultaneously. It is important to write out each timeline in detail. As soon as you schedule a contractor, repair, or delivery, you will need to write it down.

How to Maintain and Track Multiple Deadlines

There are a few things you can do to maintain and track multiple timelines. The first thing you can do is keep everything on one calendar. While you might be tempted to keep a calendar for each property, that can actually lead to more confusion. Use one planner that allows you to see monthly views as well as weekly views. Then you can choose a highlighter color to coordinate for each property. Write everything on the calendar and then highlight it with the color that coordinates with the house each appointment is for.

Another thing you can do to maintain multiple deadlines is to use an online calendar app to set up reminders each day. This will remind you of meetings or appointments on the day of, in case they are things you need to be at the house for.

Finally, another thing you want to do is check in on properties daily. Contact contractors to see how the day went and what they accomplished. If you have several houses being worked on simultaneously, it is best to have people who work directly for you at each property. They can provide daily progress reports, as well as contact you throughout the day with updates on renovations, deliveries, and more.

Coordinating Contractors to Work on Multiple Houses

Talk to your contractors about the work that needs to be done at each property. If you plan to have the same contractor working at multiple properties, set up a schedule with him as soon as you have the keys to each property. Giving the contractors as much notice as possible will increase the likelihood of them being able to work with you.

Staying on Top of Multiple Projects

The easiest way to stay on top of multiple projects is by not letting things pile up. When a task needs to be done, just do it. If materials need to be bought, go buy them. File your paperwork each night. Check on all your properties each day. Return phone calls as soon as you can and check-in with your contractors daily. You cannot give in to procrastination.

Supervising Multiple Budgets

In addition to coordinating and tracking multiple timelines, you will also need to coordinate and track multiple budgets. Each house will have its own budget, and you will need to track expenses separately in order to properly determine profit and expenses. When it comes time to file your taxes, your accountant will want to know which house each expense can be attributed to. Tracking expenses properly as they occur will save a great deal of time and money when filing your taxes. You can save money by minimizing the number of hours you will need to pay your accountant. The longer it takes the accountant to organize your expenses, the more you're going to pay.

How to Maintain and Track Multiple Budgets

It is important to keep a project binder for each house you are working on in order to keep everything organized. As part of this binder, you can have a large envelope in the front pocket to catch receipts throughout the day. This will keep you from losing receipts. The downside to this method is that you may be buying things for multiple houses on one receipt. At the end of each day, go through the envelope and record the expenses in the appropriate budget. Go through the receipts and highlight the items that go to different houses.

How to Save Money with Multiple Projects

One fairly simple way to save money on multiple flips is buying supplies and materials in bulk. You can order directly from suppliers, and you can order larger quantities on things you will be able to use at all the houses. For example, light switch covers, new switches, light fixtures, light bulbs, and screws are all examples of things that will be used in most houses and can be bought in bulk.

Recording and Paying Taxes

Flipping houses will hopefully increase your annual income, but even if it doesn't you need to record buying and selling houses. Everything needs to be accounted for even if you don't turn a profit. In addition to recording everything, you will need to group everything together into categories. For example, you can't just claim expenses and throw in a number. You need to be able to break down the total number by what exact expenses you have incurred.

Maintaining Documentation

It is essential that you maintain all receipts for everything you spend. You cannot claim something as a deduction unless you can prove where and when you spent the money. If you lose receipts, you will lose deductions, which costs you money. Deductions take away from the total amount you are taxed on. Without deductions, you are going to pay more in taxes. It is essential that you keep all your receipts and records of expenses.

Hiring an Accountant

When you start flipping houses, your tax filing obligations are going to increase dramatically. You need to have a firm understanding of the tax laws and what is expected, or you could end up having to pay a lot of extra money. You could be paying too much in taxes, but you could also be paying fines for filing things late, filling out the wrong paperwork, or any other mistake. The best thing you can do is hire an accountant. Find an accountant that has worked with property investors before and understands the business. An accountant that has personal experience in property investing is even better, if you can find one.

Knowing When You Need Extra Help

If you are growing to the point where you can take on multiple flips simultaneously, you are going to feel pulled in a lot of different directions and it will quickly get too hard for you to handle everything yourself. Although it will increase your expenses, you can be more efficient and productive by hiring people to help you.

The first thing you will need to figure out is what kind of people you will need to hire. A good place to start is to figure out exactly where you want to be spending your time while working on your flips.

Ask yourself the following questions:

1. What do you feel your strengths are with your business?
2. What tasks do you enjoy doing most?
3. Which tasks make you feel the most accomplished?
4. Which tasks do you enjoy doing, even if they take a really long time?

Answering these questions honestly will help you identify where your true strengths lie. While most people assume strengths are simply the things you are good at, they are actually a combination of the things you are good at and the things you enjoy doing most. When you don't enjoy a task, you tend to procrastinate and work inefficiently.

Once you have a list of the tasks you are going to handle yourself, you need to make a list of all the remaining tasks that need to be accomplished. Group those tasks into categories that can be accomplished by one person. For example, if you have a long list of tasks that would fall into the category of clerical, bookkeeping, errands, etc., you may want to look into hiring an assistant to handle all of those for you. If you really just don't like having to check up on crews all the time, you can hire a foreman to oversee the day-to-day renovations and to make sure everything stays on schedule. If you've been doing a lot of the smaller repairs at the houses, but you want to free up your time to focus more on the business side, you can hire a handyman to go from house to house completing the smaller renovation tasks.

Hiring Employees

Once you decide what kind of positions you want to fill, you will need to create job descriptions for each position. To do this, you will then need to create a list of tasks that person will be responsible for and the past experience that you think will be most helpful for someone trying to accomplish those tasks. The list of tasks and qualifications will be your job description, which you will use to market the open position and to make hiring decisions.

Once you have your job descriptions, you can start looking to hire. Good places to post your job ads include local newspapers, Craigslist, and employment websites like Indeed.com. Be prepared to get an avalanche of applications. For each position, gather all the applications or resumes you receive. The first thing you want to do is quickly go through and eliminate all the ones that are clearly not the right choice. This may include applicants who did not provide the requested information, did not present a professional application, do not have the experience you are looking for, and those who did not appear to have even read the job ad. This will leave you with the short list of applicants to actually read through carefully and decide who you want to interview.

ALERT

While it is tempting to hire friends or family members to fill in a job position for you, there are complications that come with this decision. You need to ask yourself: If they aren't working out, will you be able to let them go?

Managing a Staff

Once you have employees working for you, you will need to add staff management to your list of things to do. You'll need to work out what is expected of them on a daily basis, how you will monitor their performance, and more. Managing other people is a skill all on its own; if you find you are having trouble with this aspect, it is good to seek guidance from other people in the business who have employees.

However, the best approach is to be clear and honest about your expectations and hold people accountable for their work. You also don't want to micromanage. If you hired someone and their performance leads you to feel they need to be micromanaged, then they probably weren't the best pick for the job.

Encouraging a Team Atmosphere

Generally speaking, people perform better when they feel appreciatcd. While it is always important to maintain your position as the boss and leader of the company, encouraging a team atmosphere can go a long way in encouraging increased productivity. You can help create a team atmosphere by having team meetings. Use these meetings as an opportunity to see where everyone is at in their tasks and what their goals are for the week. Weekly meetings are also a great opportunity to point out the good work people are doing and the things the company as a whole has accomplished together.

Working with Freelancers

Hiring employees can be stressful and expensive. You will have increased tax obligations, increased paperwork, and more. While having solid employees can make your business run smoother, they are also a commitment. Another option is to work with freelancers. Freelancers work as independent contractors, which means they only work when you have work to give them. If business slows down, you aren't under any obligation to provide work for freelancers.

You can also outsource work virtually. While this won't work with your handyman, if you need an assistant, or help with tasks like online marketing or bookkeeping, you can hire a virtual assistant. There are a lot of people who work from home as virtual assistants. A lot of these people also work as freelancers, so you only pay them for the workload you need completed.

Creating a Brand

By the time you are doing multiple flips, you have, hopefully, worked to create a brand. Your brand would include your company name, logo, website, marketing materials, business cards, etc. You want to work toward being known as a property investor in the area. When people know who you are, you have a better chance of good deals coming to you. Banks will be interested in working with you to unload their REOs. Other investors and prospective buyers will be coming to you looking for properties. There are two ways you can accomplish this: marketing and reputation.

Marketing Your Company

You need to market your company with the same enthusiasm and vigor that you would market the individual houses you are working to sell. You need to understand that your long-term viability as a company depends on how well you learn to sell yourself and your brand. Some good strategies to utilize include having your own yard signs created. Pass out business cards whenever the opportunity arises. Make sure you have a solid online presence. Use a lot of images and videos to promote your houses and your company. Marketing, itself, can be a full-time job. If this is not one of your strengths, it is a good thing to delegate to a qualified employee.

Developing a Good Reputation

The second way for you to create and market your brand is by building a good reputation. If your houses are consistently well-renovated, reasonably priced, green, or a combination of these qualities, you will develop a reputation for it. Interested buyers will seek you out because they know you sell quality homes, and you won't try to hustle them. While developing a good reputation takes time, it is also highly effective and long-lasting.

Managing an Office

When you are operating at a larger scale and flipping multiple houses, a dedicated office space is essential. You will need a dedicated work area to do paperwork, make phone calls, prepare estimates, and more. You will also need appropriate filing space and room for a fax and scanner. In addition to an office, you will also need room to store things: materials and supplies that are either extra or not ready to be used yet, as well as tools, equipment, and more. Running a house flipping business requires space to work.

Over 10 percent of Americans work from a home office. That number has increased dramatically in the last ten years. The advancements in technology have made it more possible for people to effectively complete their work from home.

A Home Office

A lot of house flippers start working out of a home office, and there is certainly nothing wrong with that. A home office provides the comfort of being able to work from home while also having a separate space to work. A home office also provides you the flexibility of being around when you are needed.

Despite the benefits, a home office does have its disadvantages. You may have too many distractions trying to work from home. If you have kids, you may have a hard time keeping them out of your office, especially when you are working. Additionally, working from a home office often makes people feel like they never really get to leave work.

In order to make a home office work, you need to set a few boundaries. Family members need to understand the importance of not invading your home office and touching or moving things. They also need to understand that when you are working, you need to focus on work. One way to reinforce that is to set business hours. Decide what hours you will be in your office working, and you can't be disturbed during these the hours. However, when business hours are over, you will participate in what is going on in the house.

When to Move Out of the Home Office

Even if you find success with a home office, you may reach a point where you need more space. Having a business location will make it easier for you to hire employees and have them work with you at your office. It will be easier to schedule meetings at your office. It will also be easier to create storage space. You can find a location that includes a large backroom or small warehouse. You can use the storage space for your tools, equipment, supplies, and materials. This will also make it easier for your contractors or handymen to pick up things they need for a job. Finally, this will also create a clear separation between work life and home life.

CHAPTER 18

House Flipping Tax Requirements

When flipping houses, it is essential that you maintain proper documentation and pay all the appropriate taxes. Making mistakes with your taxes can be very costly, and the IRS does not accept ignorance as an excuse for mistakes. It is essential to have a basic understanding of your tax obligations and to have a qualified accountant on your team to ensure everything is taken care of properly and on time.

Paying Property Taxes on Flipped Real Estate

When you buy a property, you take on responsibility for the property taxes. The property taxes will be determined by the area where the house is located. There are a wide range of factors that go into how much you will pay in property taxes. The amount you will owe in taxes will be disclosed prior to officially buying the property. This is information you can gather online while you are still researching possible properties. Once you own the property, if you feel the tax value of the property is too high, you can request reevaluation. However, the rules regarding having a property reevaluated vary by area, so you will need to research the regulations for your area.

Understanding Your Tax Commitment

Regardless of how quickly you resell a property, you are responsible for the property taxes that collect while you own it. This can be a relatively small amount if you flip the property quickly. People new to flipping houses often overlook a wide range of expenses; this is part of the house flipping learning curve. Property taxes on the investment property tends to be one of the expenses that goes overlooked. People assume they're going to sell the house so quickly that it won't matter. This is often not the case.

Payment Options

If you bought the house with a bank loan, there is a chance you will need to pay the property taxes on a monthly basis along with the mortgage payment. If this is not the case, they will need to be paid every six months. It is very important to stay current on all property taxes. Otherwise, you may have a large bill to deal with that includes late fees, which can be hefty.

Working with an Accountant

When flipping houses, it is essential to have a qualified accountant as part of your team. It is best to have the accountant before you even buy your first property. This way, you'll be able to hit the ground running. There are many possible tax implications you need to be aware of when flipping houses. How much you pay and which taxes you pay will vary depending on how much you make, how fast you sell properties, the state, city, and county you live in, the location of the house, and more. Filing these types of business taxes is not a simple task, and it is certainly one you should leave to a professional.

QUESTION

If I have a home office, can I deduct things like electricity and gas? This is a common question and one your accountant can help you figure out. Generally speaking, you will need to provide the square footage of your home office, as well as the square footage of the entire house. Your accountant will then calculate the percentage of the house that your office takes up and apply this percentage to the utility bills to figure out the appropriate deduction.

Essential Documentation

Although your accountant can help you brainstorm possible deductions, the best place to start is by keeping receipts for every dollar you spend. You want to keep receipts for stuff bought specifically for the house. You want to keep receipts for any and all business supplies: pens, paper, highlighters, paper clips, etc. You need to keep receipts from business lunches and meetings. If you meet your contractors for lunch and pay, keep that receipt. You can write off the lunch as a business expense.

Another important thing people overlook is mileage. If you don't track mileage while you are driving, you'll have an extremely hard time remembering it later. Some simple strategies to help track your mileage include writing everywhere you go on a calendar. Then at the end of the day or once a week, you can figure out your business mileage for the week. If you are only running business errands during the day, write down your mileage in the morning when you leave your house, and write it down again when you get home. The difference between the two numbers is your mileage for the day.

Your accountant can also help figure out your deductions for things like a home office, cell phone, shared vehicles, and other expenses that may qualify as a business deduction. Even if you can only deduct part of a cell phone bill because you use the phone for personal calls also, the more deductions you have, the less taxes you will have to pay.

Oftentimes, when people get in trouble with the IRS and get audited, it is because they were deducting things that aren't considered deductions. It is important to work closely with your accountant on figuring deductions.

Estimated Taxes

After you've been in business flipping houses for a full tax year, you may have to start paying estimated taxes depending on the amount of money you're making. Estimated taxes are based on your projected income for the year based on your previous taxes and your business growth. If you end up paying too much, you will receive a tax refund after filing. If you didn't pay enough, you will receive a bill for what you still owe. Once again, it is important to work with an accountant to figure out estimated taxes. Estimating them wrong or not paying them at all will result in a fine.

Avoiding Fees

There are a wide variety of ways you can get fined by the IRS. You can get fined for filing late, not filling out the correct paperwork, and not paying enough. A qualified accountant will help to ensure you avoid all possible fines and fees. Even if you are going to be filing late, your accountant can file for an extension for you. Fees are always avoidable, and doing so will make your business more profitable.

ESSENTIAL

When looking for an accountant, be sure to ask who will be responsible for the fees if they make a mistake. Some accountants will guarantee their work and cover the fees if they make a mistake.

How House Flipping Affects Income Taxes

There are a number of misconceptions regarding how you are taxed on flipped houses. The money you make from flipping houses will be figured in as part of your total income. The profit from flipping houses will be the amount left after all the appropriate deductions are subtracted. Many people assume you pay capital gains tax on flipped houses, however, that is only in very specific situations. Depending on how much you make, you may have to pay self-employment taxes on the money you make from flipping houses. It is very important to consult with an accountant regarding what taxes you will be responsible for. You should talk to your accountant sooner than later so you can be prepared if you end up having to pay taxes out of pocket.

Refiguring Your Total Income

Your total income will include all your sources of income. If you have a regular job, where you receive a W-2, you will need to provide your W-2 to your accountant along with all your paperwork for the houses you have flipped in the previous calendar year. Your buying and selling paperwork for each house will be used to determine how much was made on each property. All the deductions you recorded and tracked during the process will be taken out. A trained accountant should have no difficulty putting this together for you.

Investment versus Business

If the IRS views your house flipping as an investment, you will have to pay capital gains on the profit you made. However, if the IRS views your house flipping as a business, you will need to pay income taxes, as well as self-employment taxes. The difference between viewing it as an investment or a business is essentially based on the number of houses you flip in a year. However, there is no clear cut answer to how many you are able to flip. The IRS is intentionally vague on this point, so they have the discretion to label your activities as either an investment or a business.

FACT

The investment versus business issue is a hard one. If you are declared a business, you pay significantly more in taxes. However, the only way you're going to make a significant amount of money is to make it a business.

Capital Gains Tax

Capital gains tax is a tax assessed to the profit on the sale of house. However, while a lot of people assume this automatically applies to house flipping, it really doesn't. Long-term capital gains tax was put in place for personal residences or houses owned for a longer period of time. The only time long-term capital gains tax would apply to a house you are flipping is if you own the house for over a year.

The downside is that long-term capital gains tax is a lower percentage than income tax, which is how flipped houses have to be claimed for tax purposes. It would be beneficial to property investors to only have to pay capital gains tax, but that would mean holding on to properties for longer periods of time. This could be applicable if you end up renting out the property for a while before finding a buyer for it.

There is another situation where you will need to pay capital gains tax, and that is if the IRS views your house flipping as an investment instead of a business. In this situation, you will likely have to pay short-term capital gains, which is more than the long-term capital gains tax discussed previously.

Self-Employment Tax

Self-employment taxes are for people running their own business. Self-employment taxes are higher because they take into account taxes that are usually paid by an employer. If you start hiring people to work for you, you will also need to pay a payroll tax and a multitude of other taxes and fees associated with having employees. What you need to pay and how much you pay will depend on how many employees you have. Additionally, state taxes will vary depending on where you live. Once again, a trained accountant in your state will be able to walk you through the paperwork and ensure you have everything completed correctly and submitted on time.

The Real Costs of Doing Business

There are certain costs that are inevitable when running a profitable business. For example, paying an accountant and a lawyer are part of doing business. You can't view these types of expenses as optional or unneeded. They are an investment in the success of your business.

Tax Risks

There is a wide range of tax risks to consider. For example, depending on how much money you make on the house, you may end up losing a good portion of it to taxes. Depending on the factors of the sale, you may end up paying a type of capital gains that is assessed to short-term property investments when the money is not being reinvested. These are all tax risks that your accountant can help you figure out how to avoid. While you never want to evade paying taxes, your accountant can help you find ways to pay as little as legally possible given your specific situation.

ESSENTIAL

Talk to your accountant about the 1031 Exchange before you start flipping houses, so you have a clear understanding of your goals for your buying and selling timeline.

1031 Exchange

Many house flippers take advantage of the 1031 Exchange option in the IRS tax code. The 1031 Exchange states that if the profit from the sale of a house is reinvested into another property, you can make a tax-free exchange. Simply put, you would be eliminating the tax liability of the first property and transferring your liability to the second property. However, you can keep applying the 1031 Exchange and continue flipping houses. The tax liability exchange won't end until you stop the cycle of investment.

While this sounds well and good, there are a few things you need to be aware of. First, the IRS has very strict rules and deadlines regarding the use of a 1031 Exchange. The fact that you plan to apply the 1031 Exchange to a new property purchase needs to be declared prior to the house being purchased. Additionally, the second house has to be fully purchased within 45 days of the previous house being sold. Once again, it is very important to have a qualified accountant working with you to ensure everything is done properly and on time, so you can avoid paying extra taxes.

Choosing Where You Flip Houses

If you are a mobile person and open to moving, you can also choose to seek out an area where house flipping is highly profitable and the tax requirements would work in your favor. While you can't get away from federal taxes, you can choose states and cities with lower taxes or more lenient tax requirements. While moving to another state is not an option for everyone, it is still an option.

CHAPTER 19

Legal Regulations

There are a wide range of legal regulations you need to be aware of before flipping any houses. These regulations range from federal regulations regarding funding to local regulations on property safety. Understanding and adhering to all applicable laws and regulations will allow you to avoid unwanted fines and delays on your project. It will also keep you from jail, court costs, and negative publicity.

Legalities of Buying and Selling

Whenever you buy or sell a house, you are entering into a legal contract with another person. You legally agree to a price, who is going to pay what expenses, when everything will be paid, when the property will change hands, etc. Both the buyer and seller agree to pay any applicable taxes on their end of the deal.

Getting Help with the Legal Stuff

There are specific legal forms, disclosure agreements, and contracts that must be properly signed and notarized in order for them to be legal. There is a procedure for transferring titles that needs to be followed. The legality of buying and selling a house is one major reason many people choose to work with a realtor. Realtors know exactly what needs to be done and in what method.

ESSENTIAL

The fees associated with a realtor and title company are part of the closing costs. Who actually pays the closing costs can be negotiated along with the selling price.

Before being transferred, the title will go through the title company. The title company will go over it to make sure everything is in order. They will make sure everything is ready to be signed, and they will oversee the transfer of the keys for the property. Aside from using a realtor, you may also choose to work with a lawyer that is familiar with real estate law. A lawyer can represent you to other buyers and sellers, as well as guide you through the process properly.

Regulations in Funding

Regulations regarding the funding of houses has become stricter due to the economic upheaval in 2008, surrounding the housing market. Years of illegal mortgage lending practices came to a head when suddenly people all over the country were losing their homes to foreclosure. In addition to stricter laws and massive class action lawsuits, this also resulted in a glut of homes on the market.

FHA Anti-Flipping Regulations

The Federal Housing Administration (FHA), for a long time, had regulations in place that prevented people from flipping houses with an FHA loan. These regulations were put in place because a lot of people were conducting business in an unethical and borderline illegal way. In addition to other issues, people were reselling houses before the official closing date of their purchase. They were selling houses at a significantly higher rate without doing any actual work to the house, and many were reselling them quickly due to acts of mortgage fraud. The FHA tried to eliminate the potential for fraud and unethical practices by making it hard for the investors who were responsible for these unethical dealings to get a loan.

HUD's Waiver of the Anti-Flipping Rule

HUD stands for the U.S. Department of Housing and Urban Development. Although the FHA regulations were put into place to protect the market and potential buyers, following the 2008 market fiasco, something had to change. In addition to the glut of houses forced onto the market, thousands of former homeowners were now unable to get a mortgage loan due to their foreclosure.

HUD decided to introduce a temporary waiver to the anti-flipping rules that would allow investors to flip houses with FHA loans under five clear and specific conditions. These conditions were put in place to dramatically decrease the potential for fraud or unethical dealings with the properties being flipped.

The original anti-flipping regulations included a clear regulation that houses could not be resold within ninety days of purchase. Additionally, if a house was resold between 91–180 days after the original purchase at a new selling price that was 100 percent or more of the original selling price, the seller had to provide documentation to the FHA verifying the value of the property.

The waiver did away with the ninety-day wait period to resell a house. This allows house flippers to buy a house with an FHA loan and then renovate it and resell it within a three month period. There are five conditions applied to these situations that house flippers need to fulfill before they can resell the house.

FACT

As the housing market improves, the HUD waiver will be eliminated and the FHA guidelines regarding flipping properties will return to the way they were. It is not clear when the waiver will be eliminated.

Second Appraisal Is Required

If the house is going to be sold at a profit of 20 percent or more to the seller, the FHA requires the seller to provide a second appraisal by a different appraiser. This is to confirm the accuracy of the first appraisal. The seller also needs to provide verification of the completed repairs and renovations that were made to the house, which led to the increase in value. Finally, the buyer is not allowed to pay for the second appraisal. It is typical for the cost of an appraisal to fall on the buyer, and while the buyer may need to pay for the first appraisal, the seller has to pay for the second appraisal.

A Home Inspection Is Required

The seller is expected to have an inspection of the house, prior to it being sold. The inspection has to be done by someone that has no relation or connection to the seller. The seller has to be the one that pays for the inspection. Any needed repairs discovered by the inspector have to be completed and paid for by the seller before the house can be sold.

Health and Safety Repairs Must be Completed

Any and all health and safety repairs will need to be completed before the house can be sold. Additionally, if the house had already been appraised and additional needed repairs were discovered by the inspector, after the repairs are made, the house will need to be appraised again. The seller will need to pay for the additional appraisal, and the appraiser will need to make note of whether or not the repairs were made.

No Conflict of Interest Between the Buyer and Seller

The FHA refers to this as "arms-length" transition. There can be no connection between the buyer and seller or any other entities involved in the transaction. This includes escrow and title companies. For example, if a property investor also owns an escrow company, they cannot use their own escrow company in the transaction. They have to choose a different company. The possible conflict of interest is an important point for the FHA because it is these types of connections that allowed so many illegal transactions to happen in the first place. The FHA will investigate any possible connections between parties involved.

A Twelve-Month Chain of Title Is Required

The FHA also requires a twelve-month chain of title. This will reveal how many times the title has been transferred and at what prices. If a house has been flipped twice within a 12-month period, it will not be eligible for FHA funding. This is to get houses out of the flipping cycle that have been used in previously unethical situations. If a house has been flipped multiple times within a twelve-month period, it is unlikely that the previous flippers made the needed renovations. This was often accomplished by artificially inflating the value of houses.

ALERT

Finding a property that has been flipped multiple times in less than a year is a clear indication that mortgage fraud has been involved. Regardless of whether or not you are working with an FHA loan, it is best to stay away from these properties and the people trying to deal them.

What Impact the Waiver Has on House Flipping

The HUD waiver has opened the door for house flippers to do business with the help of FHA loans. If a house flipper is doing her job ethically and to the best of her ability, there should be no concern regarding the five regulations placed on flipping houses. When flipping a house with an FHA loan, it is important to maintain all documentation of repairs. This will help during and after the inspection and appraisal process. If there are any questions regarding whether or not specific repairs were made, you can provide documentation of the repairs.

Local Regulations to Consider

Every city has its own set of rules regarding everything from property maintenance to building codes and garbage disposal methods. If you are flipping a house in a city other than where you live, it is very important to get acquainted with the local regulations that may pertain to the property you want to buy. Getting fined by the city for easily avoidable situations is a waste of money and it takes away from the profit on the house.

Lawn Maintenance

Lawn maintenance is a common regulation in most cities. Cities will declare a certain length the grass cannot go over. If the grass grows longer than the allowed height without being mowed, the owner can be fined several hundred dollars. Even though you are busy renovating the house, it is important that you still abide by these types of regulations. Spending a couple of hours to mow the lawn once a week is worth not getting fined several hundred dollars for each offense.

Condition of Property

Most cities also have regulations regarding things like peeling paint, gutters, windows, outbuildings, etc. If these items are part of your renovations, you need to go talk to the city building inspector ahead of time. Let the inspector know your plans with the house and the timeline you will be working with. Creating open dialogue is a great way to avoid fines and citations. Typically, the city is happy to have people improve the condition of otherwise abandoned properties. However, if you don't discuss the situation with the inspector, he may not be aware of the fact you are planning to renovate the house.

Garbage Disposal

Garbage disposal days and methods is also a big concern for most cities. The first thing to find out is what days the garbage is picked up. The second thing you want to find out is how much garbage you are allowed to put out and what items you are allowed to put out other than what can fit in bags. Some cities don't care, and you can put out as much trash as you want. However, other cities are very picky about what is allowed to go out. If you are restricted by how much you can throw out, you do have other options. You can check for any regulations concerning having a dumpster on the property. You can also look into the location of the local landfill and what the requirements are for dropping off loads of trash at the landfill.

FACT

Some cities also have drop-off days for large trash items or materials considered hazardous like tires, car batteries, used oil, etc. Check with the city to see if there is an available program like that.

Building Codes

The house you are flipping will need to be up to date on multiple building codes. This may include codes related to the electric, plumbing, foundation, drainage, etc. Some cities require special inspections to ensure codes are being followed. Some cities will require that you have certified professionals doing certain jobs. It is important to understand the building codes prior to doing the work. This will prevent the need for work to be redone because it wasn't done correctly the first time or it wasn't done by the right person. Violating building codes can result in fines, as well as the final sale being delayed.

Building Permits

The requirements for building permits vary by city, so it is important to learn the regulations and laws in the city where you are flipping houses. Claiming ignorance will not stop you from getting fined if you are caught breaking the rules by not having the correct building permits. It is also important to know that there may be a fee to get the permit you need. Regardless of whether or not you think that is fair, that is the way it goes.

Why Getting the Proper Permit Is Essential

Getting the proper building permits is important for a few reasons, but truly they all boil down to the same reason: it's the law. Every city has its own set of laws and regulations regarding building and renovating. It is important to respect the laws and regulations of the city, even if it isn't the city where you live.

Getting the proper permits will help to keep you in good graces with the city officials and city building inspectors that you may need to work with from time to time. Additionally, many cities have fines in place for people caught doing work without the proper permits. This means that simply following the rules will save you money. As mentioned, there may be a fee to get the permits. However, the fee is generally less than the fine will be if you don't get a permit.

Having the proper permits is also important for tax reasons. Many areas have different local taxes. Some have city taxes and some have regional or county taxes. It is important that you keep all relevant documentation related to the work you do for tax purposes. Building permits are further documentation of work you had done on the property.

How to Get the Proper Permits

Building permits are generally handled through the building department. Very small towns may simply operate through city hall. It is important to investigate where you will need to go for permits when buying a property. Once you find the right place, you will need to fill out a request form, which will likely ask you to detail the work being done that requires the permit. If there is a fee, you will need to pay that prior to getting issued the permit.

Partnership and Investor Contracts

All partnerships or investor relationships are legal relationships. Having a legal contract drafted and looked over by lawyers will ensure that both parties are entering into the relationship with the same objectives and understanding of the relationship. The contract should detail everything from level of involvement, how spending decisions will be made, what percentage of the profit each person will receive, and more.

QUESTION

What is the difference between a partner that contributes money and an investor?
Generally speaking, a partner contributes more than just money. They contribute expertise, manpower, support, and resources. An investor only contributes money. While they may want a say in decision-making, they are primarily the money source.

Handling Disputes

Even after extensive discussion prior to entering a legal relationship, disputes happen. When there is a dispute between you and a partner or an investor that can't be resolved through conversation, you have to refer to the conditions of the contract to settle the dispute. If a dispute went to court, the judge would look at the conditions of the contract to decide who is in the right. To save the time and effort of going to court, you should start by referring to the contract to settle the dispute.

Ending the Legal Relationship

The contract should also detail how the partnership or legal relationship will be dissolved if one or more of the parties no longer wish to work together. This generally involves assigning a value to each person's contributions. This way a price can be set for one person to buy out the other.

You also need to handle unforeseen issues. What if one person dies? In a partnership, it is common for each partner to have a life insurance policy on the other partner for their share of the business. That way, if one should die, the life insurance policy can be used to buy that person's share of the company from the family. However, in an investor relationship, you will need to work out the details of how the family will be compensated for the relationship.

Once both parties sign the contract, the relationship is legally binding, so it is essential that you are completely sure of the route you want to go before entering into a contract with one or more people.

Disclosure Statements

Disclosure statements are written explanations of a specific situation in plain English. It is important to know ahead of time what disclosures you are legally required to provide. Disclosures vary from state to state, so the specific disclosures you need to provide will depend on the state you are working in. You can discover what the needed disclosures are simply by talking to a realtor, lawyer, or spending a couple minutes researching them online.

There are some disclosures that are relatively common in most states. These include death in the home, neighborhood nuisances, environmental and natural hazards, and homeowner's association information. Even among these, the conditions of the required disclosure may vary, so it is important to do your research on disclosures.

Death in the Home

Disclosing whether or not there has been a death in the home is a fairly common disclosure requirement. However, this is a clear example of how disclosure requirements can vary from one state to another. Some states require you report any death that happened in the home, regardless of how the person died. Some states only require you to disclose a death in the home if it was a result of the condition of the property. For example, if someone drowned in the in-ground pool, it would need to be reported. Some states only require sellers to disclose a death in the home if the cause of death was murder or suicide. Some states include a need to disclose stigmatized homes—for example, if a serial killer once lived in the house, regardless of whether or not he actually murdered people in that house. Finally, and this isn't as common, but some areas require you to disclose if you have reason to believe the property is being haunted by ghosts.

ALERT

While you may not know the full details, you are responsible for passing along any information you do know. Although you can't be held responsible for what you don't know, you will need to prove you didn't know.

Neighborhood Nuisances

This one also varies dramatically by state. The basis of this disclosure is to disclose sounds or smells that are part of the area due to commercial, rural, or other things in the area. For example, the state of Michigan requires that sellers disclose if they are close to farms, landfills, airports, or shooting ranges. Other states require that sellers disclose any regular noise, odor, or smoke coming from a local business or area. Not all states have neighborhood nuisances disclosure requirements.

Environmental and Natural Hazards

This area of disclosure covers two important sections. The first part refers to disclosure of dangers relating to natural disasters—for example, if the house is located in a flood plain, wetland, former landfill site, or on a fault line; anything that puts the house at an increased risk of environmental damage. The second part refers to the disclosure of environmental concerns such as lead paint, radon gas, asbestos, or if the house had been used as a methamphetamine lab. While nearly all disclosures are decided and mandated by the state, there is one environmental hazard disclosure mandated by the federal government. All houses built before 1978 are required to disclose the possible existence of lead-based paint.

Homeowners' Association Information

Homeowners' associations often come with a myriad of rules and regulations that homeowners need to know and follow. When selling a house that is part of a homeowners' association, the seller needs to disclose all the rules of the association, the financial obligations, and any other pertinent information. There have been cases throughout the country where a home buyer sued the seller and won over failing to disclose homeowners' association information.

Repairs

Many states have regulations regarding the disclosure of major repairs. However, when flipping a house, disclosing repairs is a selling point and should be done regardless of the regulations. Throughout the renovation process, you have maintained your seller binder with all the repair information in it.

Included in this disclosure requirement is often a requirement regarding past water damage. Once again, as long as the source of the problem has been fixed and the damaged areas have been repaired, this shouldn't be a concern.

Items Not Included in the Sale

This is an important one. When staging the house, you will be bringing many items in with you. It needs to be clearly disclosed that those items do not come with the house. In addition to personal possessions, this includes window treatments and appliances. Anything you are not letting the buyer keep with the house needs to be specified. Otherwise, a deal could fall through because the buyer claims they agreed to the house thinking it was fully furnished.

Legality of Not Making Disclosures

Not offering the proper disclosures can be devastating for your business and your life. You can risk criminal charges in extreme cases, lawsuits, as well as sales falling through or being dissolved. If a buyer has a solid argument that you knew about something and chose not to disclose, they have grounds for a lawsuit. Failing to offer proper disclosure can also nullify a contract agreement, which means you could be fined and end up losing the house sale.

Mortgage fraud is investigated by the IRS Criminal Investigation unit. In addition to the mortgage fraud, those responsible are often also involved in money laundering and tax evasion.

Beware of Housing Scams and Mortgage Fraud

In most situations, the best way to avoid getting involved in a housing scam or mortgage fraud is by using common sense. If a buyer or seller comes to you with an offer that just doesn't sound right or sounds "too good to be true" take the time to think about it and consult with your lawyer. Another good way to know if you are dealing with a dishonest person is if they want to make arrangements or deals outside of the official contract. When buying and selling real estate, every aspect of the deal needs to be part of the written offer and contract. There are three common real estate fraud schemes that you should be aware of.

Property Flipping

Property flipping when the property is actually renovated and increases in value is completely legal. However, there are a variety of ways people can create a flipping scheme by creating inflated house value. They create inflated value and then sell the house almost immediately after buying it for significantly more than they paid without making any renovations to the property. This is typically accomplished through providing false documentation to the lender, as well as the potential buyer.

Getting caught up with someone pulling this scheme can be avoided by using independent appraisals and common sense. It is also good to have your lawyer look over all contracts before you enter into an agreement with someone. In most situations, the seller's appraiser is in on the scam and provides the false valuation. However, you have the right to request a second appraisal. If the seller backs out of the deal or argues the inclusion of a different appraiser, it is not a good sign.

Creating Fraudulent Settlement Statements

Another common scheme is using two sets of settlement statements. The first settlement statement includes the actual selling price of the property. While the second settlement statement includes an inflated selling price. It is the second settlement statement that goes to the lender. Since the money is given to the seller, the seller has to be in agreement with the buyer to hand over the excess money collected from the lender. The house is then resold and the new buyer takes on the inflated mortgage.

Using Fraudulent Qualifications

Some buyers will get help from a real estate agent to create the qualifications they need to get a loan. This can include creating a fake work history or credit record. In these situations, both the buyer and the real estate agent are equally at fault.

Consequences of Mortgage Fraud

Unlike breaking building code or failing to get the proper permits, this is more than just a citation and a fine. Mortgage fraud is a serious criminal offense, and is punishable by fines and jail time. After the mortgage crisis in 2008, a lot of people went to jail as a result of their involvement in this system. In order to avoid accidental involvement or being duped by a scammer, it is important to do everything by the book. Don't trust people who try to work out backroom deals. It is better to walk away from a deal that seems perfect than get involved and end up in prison.

CHAPTER 20

Facing Risks Head-On

There are a wide range of risks involved when flipping houses. However, if you are prepared for those risks, you can face them head-on. Being prepared is the best way to handle unfortunate situations. It is also important to keep your end goal in mind. Even if things don't go exactly as planned, making money is your end goal, so preserving your potential profits is essential.

Planning for Major Expenses or Renovations

Major expenses and renovations don't have to be a major risk when flipping a house if you are aware of them and plan for them correctly. If you are able to conduct a full interior and exterior inspection of the house prior to buying it, you will be aware of any major problems, and you can figure that into your renovation costs and potential profit. If you were unable to inspect both the inside and the outside, you may not be fully prepared.

Planning Costs Into Renovation Plans

Even if you are only able to conduct an exterior inspection of the property, you may be able to identify some significant potential expenses. For example, you may be able to see from the outside that the house will need a new roof or new windows. When problems are identified during an inspection, you need to plan that expense into your total renovation estimate.

ESSENTIAL

To account for unexpected expenses, add 10 percent to your estimated amount. If you accurately estimated expenses and there were no surprises, this amount will be unneeded.

You can then use that potential expense in your negotiations to buy the house. You can decide if there is enough room to make the needed renovation and still turn a profit selling the house. It is important to get an estimate for the renovation prior to buying the house. It is also important not to estimate renovation costs on the conservative side. Plan for more costs than you think will honestly be needed. This will create a cushion in case the actual expenses go over your estimates.

Mitigating Costs Where Possible

Planning ahead for renovation costs isn't always possible. Sometimes problems are worse than you thought they would be or there is a needed renovation that you weren't aware of before buying the house. In these situations, it is important to spend as little as possible in order to stay within your intended budget.

Mitigating repair costs include only doing needed repairs and making needed repairs as cost effectively as possible. For example, you may have planned to put in new kitchen cabinets, but then you found out the house needed a new furnace. In order to mitigate costs, you can choose to only replace the cabinet doors to give them a fresh new look. The money saved on the cabinets can then be used on the furnace.

Unexpected Repairs

Not all renovations and repairs need to be major. In some cases, it is a series of small repairs that cause you to go over budget. When flipping a house, there are a million little details that individually don't seem important, but when trying to market a house to prospective buyers, these details will matter.

Once again, the best way to plan for unexpected repairs is to have as few as possible. The more you know about the house before you buy it, the more prepared you will be going into the project. However, you will handle unexpected repairs the same way you will handle everything: with the end goal in mind.

Identifying the Source of the Problem

The first thing you want to do when dealing with an unexpected repair is to identify the source of the problem. This can mean a number of things. First, the repair could be an indication of a larger problem. For example, a crumbling ceiling can be a sign of water damage. Identifying the larger problem is essential to mitigating costs. Fixing the smaller problem will lead to more problems in the future because the larger problem was ignored.

Another thing to consider is if someone is at fault for the unexpected repair. For example, say you bring in a painting contractor to paint the interior of the house and one of their workers cracks the ceiling by pushing too hard with a stippling brush. The needed repair is the responsibility of the painting contractor. While you might want to be a "nice guy" about it and say "no big deal," the repair will eat into your potential profits. This goes the same for all contractors you bring into work on the project.

What if the contractor made a mistake but refuses to fix it?
Sadly, this can happen. You can attack this problem on two fronts. The first is to find and hire a replacement, so you still get your project done on time. The second is to pursue getting back any money you paid the contractor for the work that was not completed.

Making Repair Decisions

When repair decisions need to be made, you need to keep your end goal in mind. You are in this to make money, so the first thing you need to ask yourself is if making the repair is essential and will help you make money on the flip. For example, you may personally like to replace the kitchen counter. However, if the kitchen counter is in good condition and not notably outdated, there isn't really a reason to replace it. This can go the same for larger repairs. If there is a shed on the property that needs a lot of work to make it usable or safe, it may be more cost-effective to tear it down and sell the house without a shed than to repair the shed.

Unforeseen Expenses

Unforeseen expenses can be more than just repairs. Any unplanned expense needs to be carefully thought out in order to protect your potential profit. It is also important to stay calm and face each unforeseen expense head on. Simply reacting to a bad situation or making an emotional decision will be costly and likely unproductive. You want to first examine the situation and the expense, and then handle the expense.

Types of Unexpected Expenses

Unforeseen expenses can mean buying tools or supplies you weren't planning to buy. They can be costs associated with going past your deadline.

For example, if you plan for a three-day dumpster and it takes you six days to clean out the house, you will need to pay for three extra days that you weren't planning to pay for.

Unforeseen expenses may include fines from the city due to regulatory issues. For example, you may be charged extra for having too much trash, or you may be charged a fine if you do not have the correct permits for the work you are doing. Some cities have special inspections that you are required to get on home renovation projects and they cost money. Some cities also charge for things like unmoved properties or having junk vehicles on the property. Another possible unforeseen expense could be the loss of deposit on rented tools or equipment that breaks or is not returned on time. A majority of these expenses can be avoided with careful planning.

How to Handle Unexpected Expenses

The first thing you need to do is remain calm. Evaluate the expense and why it occurred. See if you can mitigate the expense by simply speaking with the powers that be. In some situations, if you just explain yourself, you can reduce or eliminate fines and fees. If you are unable to reduce or eliminate the extra expense, you may be able to set up a payment plan or work out a future deal. Going back to the dumpster example, if you need the dumpster for a couple of extra days, you can contact a representative from the dumpster company and work to develop a relationship. Explain the need for the dumpster and the prospect of future contracts if they are willing to work with you.

Contractor Fails and Mistakes

Even if you've worked with a contractor multiple times, contractors fail and mistakes can happen, and they can cost you valuable time and money. The first thing you need to do is establish relationships with contractors you can trust and you enjoy working with. Having a relationship with the contractors will minimize the risk of fails and mistakes, but it will also put more pressure on the contractors to fix their mistakes. Any successful contractor will want to maintain a positive relationship in order to secure future work.

Responding to Contractor Fails and Mistakes

The first thing to keep in mind is that you cannot react emotionally. Although it is natural to get upset when someone makes a mistake, you need to walk away and calm down before talking to your contractor about it. You also need to stop and think about the problem. Was it an honest mistake or was the contractor not following instructions, rushing, or trying to cut corners? The cause of the fail or mistake will affect how you respond to the problem.

Fairly common fails or mistakes you might encounter include the contractor not showing up on the days he is supposed to. This is often caused by contractors working on multiple jobs simultaneously. This also leads to jobs not being done on time. If you have multiple contractors lined up to get the house completely renovated on a tight timeline, and one doesn't show up on the days he says he'll be there, it can throw off your entire schedule and hold up other contractors.

ESSENTIAL

One way to simplify the renovation process is to use as few contractors as you can. If one contractor can accomplish multiple tasks, try to work it out with him. The fewer contractors you are dealing with, the fewer schedules you'll need to coordinate, and the fewer people you'll need to stay in contact with. Just make sure he has the manpower to complete all the work on schedule.

Getting Failures and Mistakes Corrected

The first thing you need to do is sit down and talk to your contractor about the failure or mistake. Make sure he is aware of the problem. For a contractor with multiple crew members or multiple crews, he may not even be aware there is a problem. Once the contractor is aware of the problem, you need to ask him what he is going to do to fix the problem. How the contractor responds to this question will dictate your next move.

If the contractor has a reasonable solution, which includes an acknowledgement that he made a mistake, it would be reasonable to give him the opportunity to fix his mistake. However, if the contractor denies the fact that he made a mistake or has no reasonable solution to the problem, it will likely be in your best interest to find a new contractor and discontinue working with the current contractor. Current behavior is the best indicator of future behavior.

Vandalism and Theft

While the house is being renovated, building materials and tools will be in the house. This can make it a target for theft. The house will also be empty, which can make it a target for vandalism. Oftentimes, when there is theft, it is of the tools or equipment the thieves are able to carry out. These items can be easily resold or pawned, which makes them desirable to thieves. Vandalism can be a completely separate issue. Vandalism is often the work of teenagers and may include them hanging out inside the house.

How to Handle Vandalism and Theft

If you encounter theft or vandalism, it is important to get the police involved so the incident is properly documented. It is also important to get an accurate list of the damage and the value of the things stolen for your insurance company. If you go to the house and suspect someone is inside the house, it is best not to investigate the situation yourself. Be safe, stay in your vehicle, and call the police.

ESSENTIAL

Depending on the area where the house is located, you may not be able to get house insurance for the property. Many insurance companies won't insure empty houses. However, your tools and equipment should be covered by your business insurance.

Ways to Prevent Vandalism and Theft

One way to avoid these problems is to ask the neighbors to keep an eye on the house for you when you aren't there. Give them your personal number and let them know they can call you if they see a problem. Another thing you can do is secure the house as quickly as possible. It may be difficult when you first start working on the house to secure it due to doors and windows being repaired or replaced. However, being able to secure the house will deter or at least slow down some vandals and thieves.

You should also avoid leaving things outside the house. If something valuable is found outside the house, the person who found it might be more motivated to try to get into the house, so all tools and materials should be secured inside the house at the end of each day. Finally, you can buy some relatively inexpensive security cameras for the property. These can allow you to monitor the property remotely, and if there is a problem, catching it on camera will increase the likelihood that the perpetrators will get caught.

Other Potential Risks

While there are several more potential risks, it is important to be ready and willing to face those risks head-on. There is always a solution; you just have to stay calm and think clearly. Other possible risks include the discovery of liens on the property, issues with neighbors, and issues with the utilities going into the house. There are a wide variety of potential problems that could arise from these situations.

Liens

Liens are debts attached to the property. When buying a house in foreclosure, it is the buyers responsibility to perform their due diligence in investigating liens against the property. A lien can also be a nonmonetary interest in the property. Without careful research, you could inherit debts attached to the property. Liens can be researched through the clerk of courts where the property is located. There are five basic types of liens you should be aware of: easements, judgments, mortgages, real property taxes, and unpaid federal and state income taxes.

Easements

An easement is the right to access the property. The most common type of easement is an easement with the utility company, which means they are allowed to access the property for line construction or maintenance purposes. Utility easements do not expire or go away. There is really nothing that can be done about them, but it is important to be aware of them.

Judgments

Judgments are liens put on the property to cover unpaid debts to a lender or service provided. Judgments are put in place by courts. The judgment can include unpaid debts, court costs, legal fees, and more. When the property is sold, the owner has to pay off the judgment before the title can be transferred. If the house is foreclosed on, the judgment lien can be removed, but it is important to look into it first.

Even though the debt is not yours, if you fail to identify a lien before buying a property, you may become responsible for the debt, regardless of how much it is. This is especially true with tax liens.

Mortgages

In many situations, homeowners take out second or even third mortgages on their house. These extra mortgages are considered liens against the property, and these have to be paid for before the title can be transferred.

Real Property Taxes

Real property taxes that go unpaid become a lien against the property. Although property owners are suppose to pay these before selling the house, if they don't, the lien stays with the property. Additionally, local governments can foreclose on a property for unpaid taxes. This means that if you buy a property with a real property tax lien, you can end up paying all the unpaid taxes or have the property foreclosed on after you buy it. In order to research possible real property tax liens, you need to check with local taxing authorities and property assessors.

Unpaid Federal and State Income Taxes

The government can file a lien against a property when the owners have unpaid income taxes. Similarly to the real property tax liens, these should be paid before the title is transferred, but the lien can stay with the property, which would make it the responsibility of the buyer.

Neighbor Issues

There are a variety of potential problems you may encounter with the neighbors. Whenever dealing with neighbors, it is important to keep in mind that these are not going to be your neighbors. You need to keep emotions out of it if you have an unpleasant encounter with the neighbors. Some of the issues you encounter may include a property line dispute, complaints about the noise or mess made during renovations, or even arguments that are rooted in a disagreement the neighbor had with the previous owner.

However, you want the neighbors to support your efforts to renovate the house. If the neighbors feel you are fixing up the neighborhood and helping to increase their property value, they will likely be helpful, when needed. This can come in handy, particularly if you encounter theft or vandalism problems. Since you won't be living in the house, the house may become a target for thieves looking to get tools or building materials that they can quickly scrap, pawn, or resell. Neighbors can help to keep an eye on the problem when you are not there.

For example, Matt Harkins has been a property investor in Lorain, Ohio, since graduating college in 2004. He learned how frustrating neighbor issues could be early on in his career. One of his first flips was a house that had a detached garage. The garage was in very sorry shape; there were holes in the walls big enough to stick your hand through. There were no utilities to the building, and it was dangerously leaning. To look at the garage, you would think one strong wind would knock the whole thing over.

He bought the property with the intention of simply tearing the garage down. However, after buying the house, he discovered the garage fell directly on the property line and was actually a shared structure with the neighbor on that side. Still thinking the issue could be resolved, he went to talk to the neighbor about tearing down the garage. The neighbor refused to agree. Mr. Harkins even offered to pay the neighbor for his half of the garage, but the neighbor refused to let him tear it down. Mr. Harkins even went so far as going to the city to see if he could have the garage declared unsafe and condemned. Nothing worked. It ended up taking him months to sell the house, and he sold it for less than planned, just to get rid of it.

City or Utility Issues

Sometimes you find there are issues with the utilities coming into the house that you will need to resolve with the utility companies. When these problems arise, it is important to get in contact with the utility company as quickly as possible. In many situations, if the problem is not life-threatening, you are at the mercy of the utility company's schedule. In some cases, it may take days or even weeks to get the problem resolved. You don't want this to hold renovations or the sale of the property.

When Your House Does Not Sell Quickly

Another risk you will take regardless of how many houses you flip will be the risk of not selling the house quickly. The key to really making money is to turn over the houses quickly. However, that requires being able to sell the house as soon as the renovations are finished. Now, if the house is fully renovated, priced well, and in a growing neighborhood, selling shouldn't be a problem. The risk is that you never know what can change after you buy the house. If the property doesn't sell, you won't make any money on the deal and you will lose the money you invested into the project. Not selling is probably the greatest risk people worry about when considering house flipping.

Selling to a Property Investor

If you are unable to sell the house to a home buyer, you may consider selling the house to another property investor or landlord. This, however, is a specialized market. Your best strategy would be to get in contact with landlords already operating in the area. Local landlord associations are a great place to start your search. Secondly, you will need to reevaluate your selling price. Landlords make their money over the long-term, so they are motivated to buy low in order to make their money back sooner. However, a fully renovated house in a growing neighborhood can also bring in higher rents, so you certainly don't have to give the house away.

If you are planning to sell to an investor, you can also rent the house out to start. This will allow you to bring in money while you look for a buyer, but it will also allow you to sell the property already rented, which may be desirable for a prospective investor. Regardless of whether you sell to a homeowner or a property investor, your goal is still to make money. While a property investor may negotiate differently than a home buyer, you need to have your bottom line already in mind.

ESSENTIAL

Managing rental properties can also be a profitable business. However, it comes with its own challenges, time commitments, and learning curve. If you decide to rent out properties when they can't be sold, you should look into hiring a management company to care for the properties for you.

Keeping the Property as a Rental

Another option is to keep the house as a rental property. You won't immediately get your investment back, but you will have money coming in on a monthly basis over time. The pros and cons of the landlord industry are extensive and consuming, so you want to fully look into the possibility before making a decision. While landlording may look like "easy money" to some, there is a great deal of work involved in owning rentals, and they come with their own extensive list of risks, financial and otherwise.

Appendix A:
Staging Checklist

CURB APPEAL

- ❑ The front of the house is clean of all debris
- ❑ The lawn is mowed
- ❑ All trees and shrubs are neat and trimmed
- ❑ The driveway is edged, as well as any walkways
- ❑ The front door is clearly visible
- ❑ The outside of the house is clean/power washed
- ❑ The areas around the entrance are freshly painted
- ❑ The house number is visible from the road

GARAGE

- ❑ Floor is clean
- ❑ All trash and clutter has been removed
- ❑ Anything in the garage is neat and organized

ENTRANCE

- ❑ Door mat is down
- ❑ There is somewhere for visitors to hang their coats when they enter
- ❑ If there is a coat closet, it is empty
- ❑ Any accessories hung on the walls are clean and dusted
- ❑ Floor is mopped
- ❑ Floorboards and moldings have been dusted
- ❑ If there is glass in the door, it has been washed

KITCHEN

- ❑ Kitchen counters are clean and clear
- ❑ All the cabinet hardware is clean and shiny
- ❑ Cabinets are mostly empty and perfectly clean
- ❑ Any accessories placed in the cabinets are neatly organized
- ❑ Floor is mopped and shiny
- ❑ All appliances are perfectly clean and shiny

BATHROOMS

- ❑ Fresh paint on the walls
- ❑ Bathroom counter is clear and clean
- ❑ Cabinets are empty
- ❑ New shower curtain is hung
- ❑ A new clean towel is placed on the towel bar
- ❑ New coordinating bath rug or mat is on the floor
- ❑ Floor is mopped and shiny
- ❑ Tub, toilet, and sink are all shiny clean

LIVING ROOM

- ❑ Walls and ceiling look fresh and clean
- ❑ Accessories are dusted and strategically placed
- ❑ Rug or carpet is shampooed
- ❑ If there is a fireplace, there are clean logs arranged in it
- ❑ Furniture is strategically arranged
- ❑ All hard floors are mopped and shiny
- ❑ Windows are clean
- ❑ Window sills and edges are all dusted
- ❑ All lamps and lighting are dusted, clean, and on
- ❑ All lights have high-wattage light bulbs in them
- ❑ There are fresh flowers strategically placed in the room

HOME OFFICE

- ❑ Floor is cleaned
- ❑ Windows are perfectly clean and clear
- ❑ All wood furniture is polished
- ❑ Lamps and overhead lights are dusted and cleaned
- ❑ All lights have high-wattage light bulbs
- ❑ Accessories are clean, dusted, and strategically placed

DINING ROOM

- ❏ Table is cleared and clean
- ❏ Chairs are pushed in
- ❏ Furniture and accessories are minimal and strategically placed
- ❏ Floor is clean and shiny
- ❏ Windows are clean
- ❏ Lights are clean
- ❏ All lights have high-wattage bulbs in them

BEDROOMS

- ❏ Carpets are all shampooed
- ❏ Beds are made
- ❏ Closets are empty
- ❏ Accessories are dusted and strategically placed
- ❏ All wood furniture is polished

BASEMENT AND ATTIC

- ❏ They are empty
- ❏ Floors are cleaned
- ❏ Any odors are eliminated
- ❏ If the basement is not "dry" there is a dehumidifier running

Appendix B:
Inspection Checklist

ROOF

- ❑ Look at each slope of the roof at a distance
- ❑ Look for sagging, uneven, or damaged areas
- ❑ Look for low-hanging tree branches
- ❑ Check for proper roof ventilation

ASPHALT SHINGLES

- ❑ Check for curling, missing, or damaged shingles
- ❑ Look for what appears to be gravel on the roof

WOOD SHINGLES

- ❑ Look for any kind of damage to the shingles
- ❑ Check for moss growing on the roof

SLATE AND CLAY TILES

- ❑ Check for damaged shingles or tiles
- ❑ Check to see if there are snow guards
- ❑ Check to see if the valley joints are filled with asphalt cement
- ❑ Check for rusted-out nails

METAL SHINGLES

- ❑ Check for damaged shingles
- ❑ Check to see if the joints are covered with roofing cement

FLAT ROOFS

- ❑ Check for safe roof access
- ❑ Check the surface for damaged areas
- ❑ Check the joints and seams for areas water could get through
- ❑ Check the drainage system to make sure it is working and adequate
- ❑ Check for proper ventilation

MASONRY CHIMNEYS

- ❑ Check for damaged masonry
- ❑ Check mortar joints for damage
- ❑ Make sure the chimney is vertical
- ❑ Check for open joints between the chimney and the exterior wall
- ❑ Make sure the chimney is at least 3 feet above the roofline for a flat roof and 2 feet above the roofline for a pitched roof
- ❑ Check the chimney cap for damage
- ❑ Check for a chimney top damper

METAL CHIMNEYS

- ❑ Check for damage to the metal
- ❑ Check to see if there is a rain cover

ROOF VENTS, HATCHES, AND SKYLIGHTS

- ❑ Check joints for gaps
- ❑ Check to see if hatches are operational
- ❑ Check skylights for missing or damaged glass panels
- ❑ Check for any signs of water leakage

GUTTERS AND DOWNSPOUTS

- ❑ What material are the gutters made from?
- ❑ Check for missing pieces of gutter
- ❑ Check for missing downspouts
- ❑ Check the pitch of the gutters
- ❑ Check to see if all the gutter straps are present
- ❑ Check for damage to the gutters and downspouts
- ❑ Check for sagging gutters
- ❑ Check for rotting trim or other signs of leakage
- ❑ Check to see if all the needed elbows and extensions are present
- ❑ Make sure the water is being directed away from the house

PAVED WALKWAYS AND PATIOS

❑ Look for large cracks and uneven areas
❑ Make sure the slope is going away from the house
❑ For the patio, make sure it hasn't settled creating a slope toward the house
❑ If there are any wood sections of the patio, check for rot and insect damage

DRIVEWAY

❑ Check for damaged or eroded areas
❑ Make sure the driveway is sloped away from the house
❑ Check the drainage for water coming off the driveway
❑ Make sure the driveway is wide enough for a car to park

EXTERIOR WALLS

❑ Check all walls for areas that are sagging, bulging, or don't appear vertical
❑ Check the window frames and door frames to make sure they are square
❑ Check for vines growing on the house
❑ Write down the type of exterior wall covering used

WOOD SIDING

❑ Make sure the bottom level is at least 8 inches above the ground
❑ Check for damaged or rotting wood
❑ Check for areas of discoloration
❑ Check all the boards to see if any appear warped
❑ Check to see if the wood will need to be repainted or restained

SIDING

❑ Write down what material is used for siding
❑ If aluminum, check for dented, bent, loose, or torn pieces
❑ Check all the joints to make sure they are tight
❑ Check to see if the siding has an insulated backer

❑ Check to make sure the siding has an electrical ground connection
❑ If vinyl, check for damaged pieces
❑ Check the panels to see if they appear wavy or blistered
❑ If asphalt siding is used, check for damaged, loose, or missing pieces
❑ Check for gapping or lifting joints

STUCCO

❑ Check for bulging, cracked, or chipped areas
❑ Check the quality of the paint
❑ Check for open joints
❑ Check for signs of moisture seepage

MASONRY WALLS

❑ Check for loose or bulging sections
❑ Check for cracked, chipped, or missing bricks
❑ Check the mortar joints for deterioration
❑ Check for signs of water seepage

EXTERIOR TRIM

❑ Check for missing, loose, damaged, or rotting trim
❑ Check the paint to see if it is faded, peeling, or blistered
❑ Check wood trim for signs of rot
❑ Check nonwood trim for cracked, torn, or loose sections

EXTERIOR WINDOWS AND DOORS

❑ Check windows for cracked, broken, or missing panes
❑ Check to see if the windows are painted shut
❑ Check to make sure the panes are secured in the sashes
❑ Check the overall condition of both the frames and sashes
❑ Check the weather-stripping around all doors
❑ Check wood doors for cracked, split, or damaged sections
❑ Check metal doors for dents and damage

- ❏ Check fiberglass doors for cracks
- ❏ Note if any of the exterior doors need repainting
- ❏ Check all window screens for holes, tears, and loose screening
- ❏ Check storm windows for damage
- ❏ Check storm doors for damage
- ❏ Make sure all doors and windows open and close properly and can be secured from the inside
- ❏ Check the caulking for areas that are damaged, peeling, or missing

PROPERTY DRAINAGE

- ❏ Check to see if the property is sloped toward the house
- ❏ Check to see if the house is located near a stream
- ❏ Check to see if the house is located in a flood plain
- ❏ Check to see what kind of drainage is already there
- ❏ Check to see if the available drainage is adequate for the property

LANDSCAPE

- ❏ Check for holes or sunken areas in the lawn
- ❏ Check for areas that will need reseeding
- ❏ Inspect the shrubs and plants to see if any will need to be removed, trimmed, or transplanted
- ❏ Make sure the landscape is not blocking any walkways or view of the house from the street
- ❏ Check the property for dead trees or trees with dead branches
- ❏ Check for trees hanging over the house that could be dangerous
- ❏ Check for trees that may be hanging on electrical wires

DECKS

- ❏ Note what material the deck is made of
- ❏ Check any masonry for damaged stone or mortar that will need replacing or repair
- ❏ Check wood for signs of rot or insect damage
- ❏ Check metal for signs of rust or damage

- ❑ Make sure the deck is properly anchored to the house and/or ground
- ❑ Check for open joints
- ❑ Check the deck supports to make sure they are solid and adequate for the size of the deck
- ❑ Check the railing of the deck to make sure it is sturdy and in good condition
- ❑ Check the steps to make sure they are sturdy and in good condition

FENCES

- ❑ Check wood fences for signs of rot or insect damage
- ❑ Check wood fences for damaged sections
- ❑ Check metal fences for damaged or rusting sections
- ❑ Check all gates to make sure they open and close properly

ATTACHED GARAGES

- ❑ Is the interior garage door at least one step above the garage floor?
- ❑ Is the interior door sealed?
- ❑ Check the interior ceiling and walls of the garage for signs of water damage
- ❑ Check to see if the interior of the garage will need to be repainted
- ❑ Is there proper drainage in the garage?
- ❑ Make sure the overhead door opens and closes properly
- ❑ Check all the lights in the garage to make sure they work

DETACHED GARAGES

- ❑ Inspect exterior walls for damage, bulging, or rotting sections
- ❑ Check the windows and doors to make sure they open and close properly and aren't damaged
- ❑ Check the roof for sagging or rotting areas
- ❑ Check the condition of the gutters and downspouts attached to the garage
- ❑ Check all the wood trim for signs of rot or inspect damage
- ❑ Check the overhead door to make sure it is operational

- [ ] Check the condition of the floor inside the garage
- [ ] Check the utilities in the garage to make sure they are properly installed
- [ ] Make sure the garage is properly vented

INSECT DAMAGE AND ROT

- [ ] Check all areas inside and out with exposed wood
- [ ] Check for termite tubes along the foundation or on fence posts
- [ ] Check for small piles of sawdust below exposed wood
- [ ] Check for clusters of small holes in exposed wood
- [ ] Check for wood that appears to be deteriorating
- [ ] Probe exposed wood with a screwdriver to check for rot

ATTIC

- [ ] Is the attic insulated?
- [ ] Check to make sure there is an adequate amount of insulation
- [ ] Check to make sure there is a vapor barrier
- [ ] Check to make sure the insulation was installed properly
- [ ] Check for proper ventilation
- [ ] Check for a working attic fan
- [ ] Check for signs of past water damage or current leaks
- [ ] Check the areas around the chimney and roof vents for signs of leakage
- [ ] Check the duct work joints to make sure there is no gapping
- [ ] Check for any makeshift electrical wiring
- [ ] Check all the rafters or trusses to make sure they aren't cracked, sagging, or bowed

INTERIOR WALLS AND CEILINGS

- [ ] Check for signs of water damage
- [ ] Check for damaged areas
- [ ] Check for holes
- [ ] Check for areas that appear to be sagging, bulging, or loose
- [ ] Take note of any missing trim
- [ ] Look for long cracks in either the walls or ceiling

FLOORS

- ❏ Check for areas that are sagging or spongy
- ❏ Check the floors to see if they are level
- ❏ Check all concrete floors for cracks or large chips
- ❏ Check for large gaps between the floor and the bottom of the wall

ELECTRICAL OUTLETS

- ❏ Count the number of outlets in each room
- ❏ Check to make sure the kitchen and bathrooms have GFI outlets

BATHROOMS

- ❏ Check for adequate ventilation and working fans
- ❏ Check all tile areas for cracked, broken, and missing tiles
- ❏ Look for signs of water damage
- ❏ Check the condition of the sink, tub, shower, and toilet
- ❏ Check all fixtures to see if they have individual shutoffs
- ❏ Check fixtures and pipes for leaks or makeshift repairs
- ❏ If there is a whirlpool, check to see if it works
- ❏ If the water is on, check the water pressure at each faucet

KITCHEN

- ❏ If there is a garbage disposal, check to see if it works
- ❏ If there is a sink sprayer, check to see if it works
- ❏ Check cabinets for missing or broken hardware
- ❏ Make sure all the cabinet doors open and close properly
- ❏ Make sure all the drawers open and close properly
- ❏ Check all the shelves to make sure they are level and fit
- ❏ Check the countertop for cracks, chips, and burns

BASEMENT

- ❏ Check for signs of water seepage or puddling
- ❏ Write down what material the foundation is made of

- ❑ Inspect wood framing for signs of rot or insect damage
- ❑ Check all the walls for damp areas, peeling, scaling, or flaking
- ❑ Check the basement floor for areas that are cracking or heaving
- ❑ Check to see if areas of the floor appear swollen
- ❑ Are there exposed pipes?
- ❑ Is there adequate ventilation in crawl spaces?

ELECTRICAL

- ❑ Check to see if there is adequate lighting in all the rooms
- ❑ Make note of any out-of-date wiring or switches
- ❑ Look for signs of makeshift wiring
- ❑ Look for wires that have been improperly connected
- ❑ Check for fixtures hanging from wires
- ❑ Check for extension cords being used to extend electricity to other rooms

PLUMBING

- ❑ Check to see what kind of drainage system is in the house
- ❑ If there is a septic tank, walk around to see if the ground feels spongy
- ❑ Check faucets inside and out to make sure they work
- ❑ Check to see what the material is in the inlet piping
- ❑ Does the house have city water or well water?
- ❑ What material are the pipes made from?
- ❑ Are the pipes in the house insulated?

SWIMMING POOLS

- ❑ Is the pool secured with a fence?
- ❑ If it is a vinyl pool, is the vinyl ripped, stained, discolored, or pulling loose?
- ❑ For concrete pools, are there areas with cracked, chipped, or missing tiles?
- ❑ Check for cracks or other tripping hazards in the concrete around the pool
- ❑ Check the skimmer weir and strainer basket

❑ Check painted areas to see if they need repainting

❑ Check the pump and heater to make sure they are operational

❑ Check to see if there is a lot of rust or pooling water around the heater or pump

❑ Does the pool have a cover?

❑ If so, check to see if there are any rips in the cover

Index

A

B

E

K

L

M

R

S

We Have EVERYTHING® on Anything!

With more than 19 million copies sold, **the Everything® series** has become one of America's favorite resources for solving problems, learning new skills, and organizing lives. Our brand is not only recognizable—it's also welcomed.

The series is a hand-in-hand partner for people who are ready to tackle new subjects—like you!

For more information on the Everything® series, please visit *www.adamsmedia.com*

The Everything® list spans a wide range of subjects, with more than 500 titles covering 25 different categories:

Business	History	Reference
Careers	Home Improvement	Religion
Children's Storybooks	Everything Kids	Self-Help
Computers	Languages	Sports & Fitness
Cooking	Music	Travel
Crafts and Hobbies	New Age	Wedding
Education/Schools	Parenting	Writing
Games and Puzzles	Personal Finance	
Health	Pets	